SEMI-NATIVE

SEMI-NATIVE

Jim Arnholz

Foreword by
Tony Hillerman

UNIVERSITY OF NEW MEXICO:
Albuquerque

Library of Congress Cataloging-in-Publication Data

Arnholz, Jim, 1944–
   Semi-native
   Originally published in the author's column in the
Albuquerque Journal.
   1. New Mexico—Social life and customs—
Anecdotes, factiae, satire, etc.   2. Arnholz, Jim,
1944–
I. Title
F801.2.A76   1986   978.9   86-11233
ISBN 0-8263-0895-3 (pbk.)

The contents of this book originally appeared in the
author's column in the *Albuquerque Journal* and are
reprinted by courtesy of the *Albuquerque Journal*.

"Baseball" first appeared in the *Albuquerque Dukes
Program*.

Contents

Foreword

It's surprising, at first, to learn that the favorite newspaper columnist of New Mexico's mild-mannered Jim Arnholz is the terrible-tempered Mike Royko, Chicago's Angry Man. Their writing styles are poles apart and the acidic attacks with which Royko lashes his town, Cook County and all of Illinois are utterly different in tone than anything readers will find in this book. But the surprise fades away when one takes a harder look at why each man has become so popular in the territory which concerns him.

First, there's the writing. Royko writes tight. Terse. Like this. No word wasted. He hates nine-word sentences. Subject and verb are plenty. Adjectives and adverbs are out. On the other hand, Arnholz, who will tell you that Royko is the greatest columnist alive, has a more relaxed view of communicating his notions to his readers, sometimes catching us up, like this, in a labyrinth of clauses, phrases, illuminating digressions and reversals so tricky that, if one ever had to translate it into Spanish, one would despair of finding the operating predicate. Yet in the only way that really counts, they are exactly alike. Each is in total command of the language. Through the words they put on paper we see exactly what they want us to see. No confusion, no misunderstanding. Clarity—in writing that's the hallmark of the master craftsman.

Second, there's that lesson we were supposed to have learned from Ralph Waldo Emerson in our high school literature classes. "Talent alone cannot make a writer," Emerson said. "There must be a man behind the book."

I put that line second because without the first, without

the talent to produce clear prose through which we see into the writer's mind, it doesn't matter much who is behind the book. He (or she) is hidden by the murky fog of convoluted, imprecise prose. If the talent to give us a clear look at Emerson's "man behind the book" is there, then the personality of that man matters a lot.

As a genre, a word which would make Arnholz flinch, newspaper columns are poor stuff to preserve for posterity. They tend to be perishable—written yesterday to be read this morning and forgotten tomorrow—losing their relevance as quickly as lettuce loses its crispness. Like a sackful of caramels, they are monotonous if consumed one after another, without the 24-hour pause which newspaper publication imposes. Arnholz avoids the first of these pitfalls by writing about matters which are perpetual, rather than timely, and by his unusual skill at fitting technique and style to the subject.

The man behind this book, and behind most of us who read him in the *Albuquerque Journal,* is what Arnholz calls a "semi-native," a transplant (from Chicago). As tends to be the case with converts, his love of our piñon country is fervent but under constant scrutiny. (In "What Did He See?" he takes a Midwesterner on the high road to Taos and then ruminates upon why this friend's primary impression was curiosity about why residents of places like Las Trampas don't clean up their yards and plant lawns. In "Semi-Native" he describes for all of us who have lived in dry country long enough to treasure water, the odd joy of watching a flash flood rumble down a dry wash. In "Fishing for Converts" he lets those of us who fish relive the moment when we discovered the glory of landing the early morning trout.) But unlike many converts, he's avoided the True Believer curse. Royko's power lies in his skill at expressing for all of us our anger, outrage and contempt at the avarice, incompetence, corruption and meanness of the world that oppresses us. Arnholz looks at the world around us fondly. Now and then his tolerance is strained by our tendency to abuse the English language, but generally the world's knuckleheadedness is more to amuse Arnholz than to provoke a fine Roykoan rage.

I have always considered the well written essay as the penultimate literary form—second only to poetry. Done with skill, the essay is like an intimate visit with its creator. Those Arnholz essays are indeed done with skill. I like the man they allow me to visit, like his attitude, like his outlook, like his wit, his humor and his tolerance. I predict you will like him, too.

TONY HILLERMAN

*This book
is for Ruth,
because she was
always on my side.*

Preface

People often ask, "What's it like to write a newspaper column?"

My answer is that writing a column is like being married to a nymphomaniac: Just when you think you're done, you've got to do it again.

I shouldn't say that's "my" answer. Another newspaper columnist, whose name I have never been able to find, said it a long time ago and I haven't heard anything that tops it. So I owe a debt of gratitude to him. I owe a few other debts, too, and I want to square up the books.

If I owned the *Albuquerque Journal,* writing a column would be a snap. Doing anything by decree usually is. But I don't own it. So I owe Tom and Bill Lang, the people who do own it. I want to thank them for the job.

I don't run the show for the people who own it, either. Jerry Crawford is the editor of the *Albuquerque Journal.* Five years ago, he made the decision to let me have a shot at this column-writing business. I appreciate that.

In the matter of editors, I must mention two: Frankie McCarty and Curt Babcock. They work with me on a daily basis. Our relationship is the standard writer-editor relationship, which is to say there are times when they cannot understand why I wrote a particular sentence and I cannot understand why they would have the temerity to question it. But if I am to be honest, I must say that on more than one occasion those questions have saved me from looking more foolish than usual.

Then there are the readers. Writers, and newspapers, wouldn't get too far without them. Because we do not live in an age of readers, I want to especially thank the loyalists who hang in there. Writers everywhere need them.

A debt of gratitude is also owed to Luther Wilson, whose idea it was to publish this book. Luther is the director of the Syracuse University Press, but he went there from the University of New Mexico Press. One day I had lunch with Luther and writer Max Evans. It was a long lunch held in the bar at Baca's Mexican Restaurant on Central Avenue. What little I remember (about the first hour or so) of that lunch was pleasant. It was at that lunch that Luther said he wanted to publish a collection of columns. It wasn't long after that day (and part of the night) in the bar at Baca's that Luther accepted the position at Syracuse, which (I suppose) was good for Luther but (I know for sure) not so good for New Mexico. I have met few people whose soul so belonged to New Mexico. Luther Wilson is a semi-native of the first order, and I hope these words so depress him that he changes his mind about Syracuse and comes back to where he belongs.

I have to thank Tony Hillerman, too. I've known him for sixteen years. We met when he was a journalism professor at UNM and I was an incoming, ex-GI college freshman. There are many things to thank him for, but the one that stands out in my mind is his honesty. If I wrote something he liked, he said so; if I wrote something he didn't like, he said so. Nobody can ask for more than that.

Finally, there are the poker players. We've met once a week for eleven years. We have become good friends. I would be remiss if I didn't say I owe the poker players a debt, too, and with any luck they'll forget how much by next week.

SEMI-NATIVE

1

Semi-Native

I'm not a native New Mexican, but I've made strides, so many strides that two years ago a native gave me a gold bumper sticker with red lettering that said "Semi-Native." This bumper sticker has brought me in from the cold, where the outsiders are. Now I'm an insider, a semi-native, fully authorized to say the word "outsider" with the disdain of a native—which is the most important part of being on the inside of anything.

When I got my bumper sticker, I thought that was the end of it, that I had covered all the bases, but I was wrong; there was something missing. But no more. I'm a member in good standing now. I have taken my place with the natives. I have become a Rainy Season Arroyo Watcher.

It's the final step in a process that began long ago. For the most part, this process involves learning how to react to certain stimuli the way the natives do. It took some time, but now my reactions are indistinguishable from a native's. When the humidity rises above 12 percent, I am one of the first to say, "Boy, sure is sticky today, isn't it?" No longer do I chuckle when disc jockeys, their voices cracking with the strain of it all, exclaim, "Humidity—you won't believe this, folks—humidity 22 percent, 22 big ones!"

Now I nod my head in agreement, because many years have passed, years that have repressed the memory of true humidity, honest-to-goodness midwestern humidity that made it impossible to walk two blocks without having your clothes feel the way they do when the dryer turns off prematurely and the laundry is still hot and damp.

I'm a semi-native, and not only do I spell *chile* right—with an *e* instead of a Texas *i*—but I eat it right, too. Chile is not chile unless beads of sweat pop up on my forehead after two bites. If my nose isn't running and my sinuses as clear as a Taos morning, I'm likely to say (with a suitably disdainful flourish), "Tourist food." Food is somehow lacking unless my face is red, my eyes tearing, and I am saying, "Isn't this great stuff?"

Food, though, is only one of many steps to becoming an insider. More than seventeen years ago, when I first came to Albuquerque, I looked out across the city and said, "What's that brown cloud? Smog?"

"No," said my guide, "Sand, and it'll be here in about thirty minutes."

(I must regretfully add that in those seventeen years since I came to New Mexico, the odds have become 50–50 that the brown cloud is smog, with not a grain of good New Mexican sand to be found.)

When the wind blows, and minute particles of Arizona blast their way through my hermetically sealed windows, I am flush with spring fever. It seems eminently reasonable now when I hear a television weatherman tell me the next day will bring thirty-five-mile-an-hour "breezes."

Before I became a Rainy Season Arroyo Watcher, I thought I had found acceptance among the natives when I was let in on the Secret of the Shadows.

Late in the afternoons of every July and August, dark clouds rolled across the Sandias, looking for all the world to be a citywide thunderstorm, but then opening to drench only selected neighborhoods. As I drove the city streets, I could see shadowy forms behind the screen doors of almost every house. The silhouettes were people, New Mexicans watching the rain, gathering to witness the spectacle much as crowds gather to watch a space shuttle blast off from Cape Canaveral.

Then came the last piece in the puzzle: the move to the house next to an arroyo. Never mind that this man-made, miles-long piece of concrete is called a diversion channel or flood channel or some other non-native technical name. It's an arroyo, concrete or not.

When the first rain came, my front door was open. I stood at the screen, watching the heavy drops of water pelt the street. Then came the rushing sound, faint at first, then a roar, like the Rio Grande pounding through the Gorge. Then came the cars, converging on the bridge across the arroyo. Adults and children clambered out and stood in the rain. They oohed and ahhed, pointing down into the arroyo.

I ran out to see what the commotion was about. It was water. Rushing, tumbling, heavy, dirty-brown, white-capped (or at least rusty-white-capped) water. Here, in a controlled sort of way, was a laboratory specimen of a flash flood, gathered in the mountains, sent rushing through channels in the Heights that would link up with larger channels that sent the roaring stream into the Rio Grande.

So we gathered to watch, standing close, but not too close, to the arroyo's edge. This water comes through at a speed and volume that quickly instills respect in the spectator. Each year during the rainy season, someone falls in one of these concrete arroyos. Sometimes the unfortunate survives, sometimes not.

Teenagers ran down the block. "Let's go! Let's go!" they hollered. "We gotta check out the arroyo!" Some darted under the cover of porches, waiting out the pouring rain before going over to the bridge. Others, wanting to see the flow build from a gentle stream to a raging river, braved the lightning and almost horizontal rain.

These were natives, or at least passionate, bumper-sticker-carrying semi-natives.

I suppose I'm getting a little carried away here. It's hard to explain. You've got to see it for yourself.

Today, late in the afternoon, when the clouds come rumbling in over the mountain. . . . Well, I'll see you at the arroyo. We'll talk.

2

Fishing for Converts

Fishing for converts isn't all that different from fishing for fish. You have to be just as patient with a convert as you'd be with a fish; and when a nibble comes, you play the convert the same way you'd play a fish; you don't let on that when it comes to fishing, the fish are an afterthought, only a small part of the package.

"Let's go fishing," he said one day at the office.

Are you sure you want to go?

"Yeah."

We've been through this before, you know.

"Yeah, I know, but this time I'm sure. I really want to go."

OK. Come by the house Sunday. Early.

"I'll pick you up first thing in the morning. I'll come by about 8."

Eight?

"Eight."

We're going fishing. We're not going to brunch. Be there at 5.

"Five?"

Five.

"Seven."

Five-thirty.

"You're kidding."

Trust me. As soon as we catch the first fish, you'll wish we had left an hour earlier. Five-thirty.

"I can't get up that early. How about if you give me a wake-up call."

Now the hook's set, see? I've maneuvered him to where all I have to do is make the call and start reeling him in. At

5:30 A.M., Sunday, the convert stands in front of the believer's house. Then comes the convert's first indication that there is more to fishing than fish.

"Boy, it's nice and cool. Really quiet," he says.

The convert shows promise, for it is indeed cool and quiet. The city, as always, is all around us, but it doesn't feel like the city. Chances are you could stand in the street, talk in a normal tone of voice, and not wake anybody up. But we don't. Instead we stand and almost whisper, right there in the middle of the street, so early in the morning that it's still dark. The quiet seems to demand the lowered voice.

We drive east on Montaño. Ahead is the dark outline of the Sandias, shrouded in a deep blue that is only the first of many blues that will continually change as the sun rises. By the time we reach the freeway the blue has lightened and the outline is sharper. Ridges and peaks stand out in bolder relief. We both know exactly what that mountain looks like, but at this time of the morning it holds the promise of something new.

"This is fantastic," the convert says. "And everybody is in bed. They're missing it."

I tell the convert it's the best time of the day. The colors in the sky blend one into another, molting, like a bird losing old feathers and gaining new ones.

On NM-44, past the Bernalillo Circle K and over the Rio Grande bridge, there is a series of hills. We top the last hill, look to the right and in an instant there is an explosion of color and mountains and mesas. Mesas that cut across the sky as if they were drawn with a straight edge. Ahead, red rock flows like an artery through a mountainside.

We turn at San Ysidro and start the climb to the Jemez. Near Jemez Pueblo, a coyote crosses the road, stops, and watches furtively as we go by.

"How about that?" the convert says. "Wildlife."

Later, as we round a curve, one of those large, four-wheel drive pickups with oversized tires and a row of headlights on the roof looms ahead. As it whizzes by we can see the driver, a young man wearing a big straw cowboy hat.

"More wildlife?" the convert asks.

High in the Jemez, we turn onto a dirt road and climb even higher. After a few miles, we stop near the stream. In the city, it's getting hot. It will be in the 90s again. In the mountains, we're shivering; we can see our breath. Towering above us is a pine-heavy ridgeline. We walk along the stream, passing through meadows that soon will have small clouds of grasshoppers leaping from mountain flower to mountain flower. The only sound is the water.

"Good Lord!" the convert says, "Life imitates a Coors commercial."

We find a spot in the stream which is crossed by three logs forming a small pool. It has all the makings of an upscale trout condo. Only two questions now remain. Are the occupants home, and if so, have they had breakfast yet?

Baited hooks settle into the slow-moving water . . . dribble below the surface . . . under the logs . . . and WHAM! They're home! And they haven't had breakfast yet! Two rainbow trout are pulled from the water and flop on the stream bank.

The convert looks at the fish. He is pursing his lips and slowly shaking his head.

"You know," he says, " . . . we should have been out here an hour ago."

3

Scaling the Heights

It's there. I can't deny it. It's right there on all the official papers; it's on the personnel directory at work; it's on the Post Office change-of-address card. It's even on the new checks in my checkbook. It sits there like a strange growth, its malignancy or benignity still in question. Right there at the end of my new address—NE.

I have moved to the Northeast Heights; I have moved to an address with NE next to the street name. For years it was SW or NW, proper, salt-of-the-earth Valley quadrants. But no more. Now it's NE.

I have left North Fourth, the world's most beautiful ugly street. My house was only two blocks from North Fourth. I have spent so much time driving down North Fourth on my way to work that long ago I decided Albuquerque's greatest claim to fame is that it's the nation's largest secondhand furniture store. North Fourth is a junk dealer's yellow-brick road.

Now my love-hate relationship with North Fourth has turned to bittersweet memories of a long-ago affair. Now I am NE. Now I must contend with this unfamiliar urge to buy a boat. And a camper shell. And put both of them in my driveway, never to leave, never to be dampened by a lake or snowed on at a mountain campsite. It will take time before I am accustomed to using my boat and camper shell as planters.

It's not that I wanted to leave the Valley. I told the real estate agent to look in the Valley. So we did. But the timing was off; the market wasn't right. The houses weren't there. Oh, there was one, I guess, but I didn't have the $92,000 for the down payment.

So we looked elsewhere, all over the city, every quadrant, and we finally found a house in NE. I fought it, though. I protested loudly. I can't do this, I said. I can't live in the Heights. I don't even know how to find the Johnny Miller menswear section at Sears. What am I going to do about decorating the house? I thought. I'll have to rent space at the flea market and sell all my Democratic family photos. The New Mexico Republican Party called at work and offered to let me borrow some Jerry Fords until I could buy my own.

When I left the North Valley, my kind North Valley neighbor heard I was having difficulty finding storage space for my belongings. He offered to help. "No problem," he said. "Go ahead and put your stuff in my garage." Then he found out I was moving to NE and when I called to tell him when I would be over to pick up my belongings, he said it was too late and that the garage sale had been a fantastic success.

Maybe it's only the fear of something new. Maybe in time I'll settle down and find myself able to make a reasonable decision about what color to choose when buying plastic flamingos for the front yard.

I knew this wouldn't be easy, but I thought I could manage it, until I heard about the gas furnace requirements in the NE. I wasn't quite ready for harsh reality as laid down by City Council candidate DeWitt Sell of the NE, who said, "If you can't afford to run your gas furnace, you shouldn't live in the Northeast Heights."

Nobody told me about that. Not my real estate agent, not my cousin who lives in the Northeast Heights, not the guy I bought the house from. I was going to ask the gas company to put me on the budget plan so I could make equal payments each month, but I didn't do it. I was afraid somebody from the gas company would see NE on my address and tell my neighbors that the new guy was on the budget plan.

But what's done is done. I've moved and now I must adjust. I'll find a way to pay my gas bill and then I'll move on to my new life in NE.

Who knows? Maybe it won't be so hard. It's only a matter of . . . adjusting.

Maybe Ron Reagan isn't *that* bad a guy . . . and maybe we *should* do something about those welfare queens who are tooling around in Coupe de Villes . . . and Jerry Falwell . . . boy . . . Jerry Falwell . . . that guy's really a card, isn't he?

4

What Did He See?

There is snow on the peaks of Truchas. Not much, but enough to begin filling wind-eroded spillways; white rivulets empty into the shadows at the mountain base. At first, I thought the snow might have made a difference; I thought that were he with me now his reaction would be different, but then I remembered it had been early spring when I brought him here; there was still snow, and he still said what he said.

It's fall now, and it wasn't then; I have to give him that benefit of the doubt. We drove this same road, but we didn't pass by the green-gold walls of cottonwood *cañoncitos*. We came down these same winding hills to Chimayo, but Chimayo snuggled under a green blanket that day, not today's shimmering yellow and red one.

Would any of this have made a difference? Probably not. I think the Midwesterner, on seeing the High Road to Taos for the first time, would say now what he said then: "You'd think people would want to clean up their yards and plant a little grass."

What did he see?

He liked the restaurant, which is fine. It's a nice restaurant, but nice restaurants can be found almost anywhere.

We drove this same road, though the poplars were budding then, not standing in an October line of fall's Roman candles. There was no clump of chamisa, squatting on the roadside in yellow relief against its dried companions whose seeds patiently waited their turn to ride the wind.

"Reminds me of Appalachia," he had said.

He liked Los Alamos, especially the neighborhood we passed

through, with its small houses, rectangular plots, and neat lawns. He liked Los Alamos.

"Now this is my kind of town," he had said.

We stopped along the way. He looked at the Sangre de Cristos and said, "That's pretty," proving, if nothing else, that he could take the hint given to him by the official state highway sign: "Scenic View."

But there were no signs in the villages with dark brown and tan houses, no sign in front of pink adobes that wore fall clothes all year round. No sign marked the landscape abutting the houses, landscape that is unchanging 10 yards or 50 yards or 800 yards or miles from the houses.

On today's trip, for once I have remembered my binoculars and I stop frequently along the road. I'm thinking about the Midwesterner as I scan the mountains and the valleys, those little pockets with their houses and churches and farmlands and animals.

On the way back to Albuquerque, I take the low road, the highway that runs along the great scar called the Rio Grande Gorge. The road dips into Rio Grande Canyon and follows the river that doesn't quite live up to its name in the fall. Layer after layer of mountain ridgelines drift in and out of a powder-blue haze. I think about the Midwesterner.

Was it control—or more to the point, lack of it—that bothered the Midwesterner? Was that it? He liked Los Alamos, with its rectangular houses built on rectangular plots with rectangular lawns. Everything was controlled, every inch of ground under somebody's control, much like his Midwest. Farmed, sodded, built on. Used.

But this canyon land, the High Road land, won't submit so readily. This land seems to say *Keep your expectations low and maybe we can make a deal.*

A lot of people find comfort in that land. It puts them at rest. Could it be that the idea of sanctuary occurred to the Midwesterner only in Chimayo, where there was another sign—*Santuario*—to give him yet another hint?

All the way through the Rio Grande Canyon, through Ve-
larde, past the apples and pumpkins and walls of blazing red
ristras, I'm thinking about the Midwesterner.

What did he see?

5

Honkers

While driving around Albuquerque, have you ever noticed how quiet it is, even downtown? I don't mean there isn't any road noise—tires squealing, engines roaring, that kind of stuff. I'm talking about an eerie, almost graveyard kind of silence. I'm talking about the absence of a noise common in most cities the size of Albuquerque. I'm talking about car horns. Nobody honks in this city. I suppose I shouldn't say "nobody." Occasionally, there is the odd honk, but this honk usually comes from someone driving a car with out-of-state license plates. Most people in this town don't honk although some wave.

Just the other day, I was on the freeway, breaking the law by doing sixty miles an hour and in a perfect position to be honked at. (Break the speed limit by a measly five miles an hour and you might as well be parked.) I had the flood channel on one side, an almost solid line of traffic on the other and about a foot away from my rear bumper was a woman in a Volvo who wanted to speed faster than I was speeding.

No honk. Dead silence. I looked up at the mirror and there she was. All quiet on the rear-view front.

I hit the gas. Because both of us quickly were demolishing the speed limit, it didn't take long before we cleared the traffic. She pulled around me and waved. It was a funny wave, only one finger. She also said something. It was a single word. It was not "hello."

But she never honked.

Neither did the guy on the Grand overpass. Two lanes were blocked by orange-and-white street-construction barriers. We were all in a line behind a slow-moving truck. This guy thought he could make it around the truck before the lanes were completely blocked off, so he swung out of line. He didn't make it. He was stuck out there, watching the rest of us plod along up the hill.

If he had honked, I'm sure somebody would have let him in. But he didn't. He waved. It wasn't a one-finger wave, though. His fist was clenched and he was flailing his arm around and saying something to everybody in line plodding up the hill.

But no honk.

I asked some friends about the unwritten no-honk rule in Albuquerque. One said it's the Code of the West: Honkers Will Be Shot. He might be onto something. Not that long ago Denver had a rash of honking-shootings on its freeways.

Another friend, a woman, tells a story that lends credence to the possibility of honkers being shot on sight, or sound.

"I was on Indian School, waiting to turn left," she said. "The car in front of me turned and I followed. Suddenly, the car stopped. I was left hanging out in the middle of Indian School. The guy in front of me wanted to turn into a pharmacy parking lot. He was waiting for traffic to clear, except there wasn't any traffic in front of him. All he had to do was turn into the parking lot. I honked. Big mistake. He jerked open his door, got out and came toward my car. I thought, *This is it. I'm going to die because I honked.* I drove around the right side of his car and got out of there. Now when I honk— if I honk—I try to do it politely. I try to put a question mark behind my honks. You know, kind of like *beep?*"

The regionalism of the No-Honk Rule was nailed down when another friend told of the day she received her first driver's license. She was driving down an Alamogordo street and saw her father coming in the opposite direction.

"I honked my horn and waved," she said. "When I got home, he was waiting for me. 'If you ever do that again, it'll be the last time you drive any of my cars,' he said. 'Horns startle people, scare 'em, make 'em cranky. Honking is plain rude. You want to honk horns? Go east. Why do you think people in those big eastern cities are all nervous wrecks?' I've gone easy on the horn ever since. I think he was trying to save me from getting shot."

Which is good enough for me. If someone waves, no matter how funny a wave it might be, I'll wave back. But no honks. You won't hear a beep out of me.

6

Manuela Got a Letter

SANTA FE—Manuela always gets right to the point. Maybe she always did, or maybe because she is closing in on ninety years of life she has learned that getting to the point saves time, or maybe she's only relaxing in one of the few luxuries—bluntness—that the elderly are allowed. Whatever it is, we are on the High Road to Taos, headed for lunch at the Rancho de Chimayo, when Manuela, as always, begins the conversation by getting to the point.

"So," she says, "what kind of b.s. did you write today?"

None, I say, but I wrote some for tomorrow.

"Oh," she says, "I thought I missed it today."

A few minutes pass and she tells a short story, a two-sentence story that might be called "Your Government in Action."

"They sent me a letter," she says. "They told me I live in a business district."

At long last, government confirmation has come for what Manuela has known for years. House after house in her neighborhood, only a few blocks off the Plaza, has lost house status and gained office status. She is one of the last to live in a house that still is a home. Manuela's neighborhood looks as it has looked for many years, but only her house and one other look the same on the inside as they do on the outside. Outwardly, the rest look like homes, but they aren't. They're offices, bought and redecorated at great expense to look homey, but offices nonetheless.

Big money moved Manuela's stores out of the Plaza, replacing them with art galleries, trendy boutiques and cafes that serve food Manuela has never heard of. She doesn't shop on the Plaza anymore. Now her daughter drives her to a shopping center. Big money moved her neighbors, replacing them with lawyers and architects. Big money knocked on Manuela's door, too, asking if she wanted to sell the house her husband built in 1924.

Manuela, always one to get to the point, told big money to take a hike. The architects and lawyers would have to wait until Manuela was in the ground before they could close in on her house.

But now, if nothing else, it's official. They sent a letter. She lives in a business district.

We stop in the Chimayo restaurant parking lot long enough to read the sign that says the restaurant is closed for repairs until the end of the month. Neither of us thought to call before we left, assuming the restaurant would be open as always. We laugh, give thanks that it is a glorious day for a ride, and head back to Santa Fe.

We drive around Santa Fe until Manuela sees a place she has lunched at ever since it opened many years ago. The restaurant has changed little since those old days. All that's different is that the restaurant was on the edge of town back then. Now it's closer to the middle.

During lunch we are talking about the uncaught killer of a Santa Fe priest, the hippies who tried to homestead an empty house across the street from Manuela, and the day, years ago, that government changed the name of Manuela's street and never bothered to tell her or any of the residents until after it had been done. Then the talk turns momentarily to Manuela's favorite newspaper, the one she never misses, the *National Enquirer*. "They couldn't print it if it wasn't true, could they?" she says, laughing. Just as the conversation turns back to her official letter, the door behind her opens and through the doorway come several restaurant customers. They are the new Santa Feans, the chic, the kind who are at the heart of the joke: How many Santa Feans does it take to change a light bulb? Three: One to change it and two to talk about how good it was before it was changed.

I have a problem; a little temperance is in order. With Manuela, the old Santa Fean, sitting across from me, and the chic ones, the new Santa Feans, standing in the doorway, I'm in danger of cooking up caricatures outfitted with designer jeans and gold chains.

The problem is that one man standing in the doorway is indeed wearing tight jeans with somebody's name on the back pocket. I'm thinking it's a good bet that the name isn't the name of the guy wearing the jeans. Another in the group has strands of gold chains draped around his neck. Thick chains, thin chains, enough metal to repair a battleship. The women are chic in jumpsuits and snowsuits and white furs.

The guy with the chains is wearing . . . these shoes . . . I figure there's only one way he could come by shoes like these shoes: He must have killed an Irish Setter and put soles on the hide. His shoes are red and furry. Footwear by Sasquatch. And if the chains aren't enough, and if the red, furry Irish Setter shoes aren't enough, the guy is carrying a purse.

Everything about these people looks expensive, conjures up thoughts about the kind of money that can take a whole town and turn it into a toy, the kind of money that sooner or later shows up as an official letter that says you live in a business district.

Manuela sits with her back to the big money, which is probably best in the long run. Remember, she always gets to the point, and the last thing I want to do is referee a discussion between Manuela and a guy with furry red shoes and a purse.

Ah, well, things change, don't they? All the crying in the world isn't going to change the change. But it isn't every day you get to see the old and new sitting five feet apart.

Manuela and I got up to leave, with me moving to her side of the table to help her up. She has a bad hip. It takes her a while to get up and down. After lunch, though, she will walk from her home in the official business district to attend Mass at the cathedral, just as she always does. Her son will pick her up after church. She doesn't like to walk home in the

20

dark. We were nearing the door, walking by the group's table when I caught just a little of their conversation.

"Have you tried sopaipillas?" the blonde in the white snow-suit said. "They're sort of like bread with a lot of air inside."

7

I Bought a Truck

I bought a pickup truck. I hope I did the right thing. I hope it's the right kind of pickup truck.

I wasn't too concerned until I saw a newspaper column written by a pickup owner who said, "If you have a pickup truck, then you are in a fraternity as solemn and deep as all the Elks, Moose and Odd Fellows put together."

I've had my pickup truck for only a day or so, but already I'm staying up late at night, not sleeping, worried about being a responsible member of the deep, solemn fraternity.

"Are you still looking for a pickup?" my mechanic had said over the telephone a few days ago. "My daughter's selling hers."

I asked him if it had dents, well aware that according to the deep, solemn fraternity, it had to have dents.

He hesitated a moment, and then said, "Nice dents."

I asked if it was old enough.

He said it was a 1971.

So far, so good, I thought. Nice dents and it was eleven years old. But I certainly wasn't going to buy a pickup truck just because it had nice dents and was old enough. There's more to the deep, solemn fraternity than that.

Does it bounce well, I wanted to know. Not exactly like a low-rider, but, you know, does it bounce like it hasn't seen new shocks since the signing of the Declaration of Independence? Does it bounce like . . . well, like a pickup is supposed to bounce?

He said it bounced exactly the way pickup trucks are supposed to bounce.

And it had a squeak, an absolutely gorgeous, hard to pinpoint, impossible to fix, definite pickup truck squeak. You could hear it when you came to a stop.

Already I was dreaming of my first red light, the first glorious squeak, a high-pitched melody punctuating a comfortable bounce. It was beginning to sound like the perfect pickup.

I asked it it had an empty beer can and a Wendy's hamburger wrapper on the floor of the cab. It said in that newspaper column that members of the solemn and deep fraternity of pickup owners all had empty beer cans and Wendy's wrappers on the floor.

The mechanic said I would have to provide those myself. The truck had been cleaned out prior to being put up for sale.

That's when the doubts began to creep in. I could understand wanting to clean a car, but what serious candidate for the deep and solemn fraternity would consider the purchase of a clean pickup truck?

What about the mirrors, I said. It doesn't have those dinky sissified car mirrors, does it?

He said it had two mirrors. Both big. Genuine West Coast mirrors.

I was feeling pretty good about this pickup truck. Nice dents. Old. Big mirrors. Good bounce. A squeak. The only negative was the lack of a beer can and a Wendy's wrapper, but that wasn't a big deal. Almost any used vehicle needs a little work, doesn't it? I moved on to the mundane but mandatory question. How does it run?

The mechanic said he had done a lot of work on it and explained what sort of changes he had made in the engine. I listened intently, not understanding a word he was saying but doing a passable job of nodding and pretending that I was with him all the way. He talked about engine performance while my mind drifted, wandering over the truck's body, trying to imagine where the dents might be.

I told him I wanted to see the pickup and take it out for a test bounce.

Now, this mechanic is an old and trusted friend. Everything

he had said about that truck was true; it wasn't until we were standing in his driveway that I noticed something he hadn't mentioned. He had opened the hood to show me the engine and explain once more what he had done to it.

"What's that?" I said, pointing to a cylindrical object that I had never seen under the hood of any car or truck.

"Oh, that's my daughter's Christmas present," he said, walking around to the car, reaching under the dash and pushing a button.

"AH-OOOOOOOOO-GAH!"

I bought the pickup. I hope I got the right kind.

8

Jimmy the Burrito Man

Jimmy is:
(a) an entrepreneur
(b) a salesman
(c) a hustler
(d) illegal
(e) all of the above

It is 8:50 A.M. Jimmy sits in a booth in an East Central restaurant.

"I'd buy you breakfast," he says, "but we haven't got time."

No time? Who eats burritos at nine o'clock in the morning?

"Finish your coffee. You'll see."

Jimmy climbs into a worn, green Chevy and drives down Wyoming. An experienced knee is positioned against the steering wheel. An experienced hand reaches into the back seat where the insulated box holds the morning's burritos. He has a small aluminum tray in the other hand and quickly fills it.

"Don't worry," he says, seeing me nervously eye the knee that is controlling the steering wheel. "I drive like this all the time. I'm pretty good at it."

An automobile dealership is the first stop. He walks at a pace that qualifies as a slow trot. The first door he approaches is clearly marked with a painted sign: "No Soliciting. Employees Only." Jimmy pushes open the door and walks into the service bay.

"Burritos!"

Some of the mechanics are waiting for him, anticipating

his every-other-day arrival. A new customer holds a dollar bill.

"What do you have?" the mechanic asks.

"Breakfast burrito! Jimmy Dean Pure Pork Sausage, scrambled eggs, and red chile."

Dollars are held out. The burrito tray is held out. Customers pick one and leave. ("I always let them take it. What else can I do? I've got the tray in one hand and money in the other.") One dollar. One burrito. ("I'm the best commercial Jimmy Dean ever had.")

Back in the car, quickly. Maybe a few seconds for chit-chat. "How did the ball game go last night?" But not too much chit-chat. Chit-chatting in the car won't sell burritos.

How come you didn't go into the showroom? I ask him. What about the new-car salesmen?

"Not at that place," Jimmy says. "They don't make enough. I go in there and they say they're broke. Can you imagine that? Can't afford a dollar for a burrito."

He drives down Wyoming, toward Lomas, steering with his knee, filling the tray, stopping at auto dealerships. Now it's into showrooms, used car lots, service bays, parts departments. At one, in the well-appointed office of the owner, a meeting is in progress involving the owner, the general manager, and the sales manager. Jimmy smiles, says hello to the secretary, and sails past the woman without waiting for a reply. He peeks around the partially opened conference room door.

"Burritos?" he asks quietly.

He sells five.

At another showroom a salesman asks, "Can you let me go for one until Monday?" Jimmy is friendly and polite and says there's no way. Back in the car he explains, "New guy. Who knows? Probably won't be there by Monday." In a service bay, a mechanic says, "Can you let me go on two until Monday?" Jimmy is polite and friendly and says, "Sure, no problem." Back in the car he explains, "Been there a long time. He'll be there Monday."

On the road again, knee at the wheel, hands filling the tray. He stops at a small plant off East Central and walks into the break room. At 9:28 the room is empty.

"Early," Jimmy says, heading for the office next door to shoot the breeze with the secretary of another firm. He sells her a burrito and goes back to the break room. It's 9:30. They're waiting for him. He sells fifteen burritos, talks about his vacation to Mexico, hurries back to the car, and starts the long drive to the North Valley, to the body shops and welding shops and other workplaces along Second Street. Along the way, he ruminates on the burrito business.

"I got into it because I was broke. Busted. Didn't have a dime. I used to own a rock band and a club in Texas. Then I sold cars. I like the challenge. I like selling anything. I don't care if it's a ten-thousand dollar item or a one-dollar burrito. I'll get out of this pretty soon. The challenge is gone. I make good money. But the challenge is gone."

He acknowledges that burrito salesmen are not listed in the social register.

"Sometimes people look at me like I'm . . . well, you know. They think I'm nothing. I don't care. I make more money than most of them. One time, at a ball game, I saw a lawyer I sell burritos to. I said, 'Hey, don't I know you?' He said, 'No.' Then he looks away. I said, 'Sure, I do. You're a lawyer.' He said, 'No, I'm not.' His wife was with him. She looked at him like he was crazy."

Jimmy stops at a welding shop, sells six, hurries back to the car. "Maybe I could have sold more, but they looked busy. I never bother people when they look busy."

He drives, quietly now, until a sheepish smile breaks across his face. "I'm illegal, you know. I don't have any of the permits or anything. I got turned in once by a guy who drives a roach coach. I was outselling him and he got mad. It's not much of a hassle to get legal, but I'm not."

If it's not a hassle, why not get legal?

The smile returns, this time accompanied by a shrug. "I

don't know. My business is clean. I use good food. And besides, what are they going to do to a poor burrito seller?"

By 12:15 he is through. Around 5 P.M. he will go to the small, low-rent apartment where two women have been turning out burritos all day long. He'll load up and head for the happy hours at East Central bars. He'll sell burritos to bartenders, customers, hookers ("Oh yeah, I know 'em all"), and topless dancers ("Great way to meet girls").

But he says the challenge is gone. He's going to get out of the burrito business. Says he hates it. And besides, he must periodically taste-test the product, a particularly grueling task. Jimmy the Burrito Seller can't stand chile. Never could. It does terrible things to his stomach.

9

Constructive Criticism

New Mexicans don't take criticism well. If the criticism is constructive, the reaction is even worse. Thin-skinned, hypersensitive New Mexicans get their hackles up at the drop of a constructively critical word.

George Martin didn't know that when he wrote me a letter with his constructive criticism for New Mexico.

"I'm a resident of Ohio, but am here for the winter," George writes. "I would like to suggest that 'Land of Enchantment' be changed to 'Land of Broken Bottles, Beer Cans, Debris, No Traffic Enforcement and Barking, Unlicensed Dogs.' I anticipate you will accept the above as constructive criticism."

Certainly I will. Nobody else will, but I will. I've been arguing for years that what this state needs is to be more like Ohio. Some people take offense at this. One New Mexican told me, "I've never been to Ohio, but I've always imagined it to be a sort of gigantic Sears store. You know, like the whole state is covered with a ten-foot roof, and one county is menswear, the next county is small appliances . . . Something like that."

That's the attitude I've run into when I say New Mexico should be more like Ohio, and that we were taking a step in the right direction with the festival marketplace idea. It's a shame it was voted down, no doubt by an electoral bloc that doesn't appreciate all Ohio has to offer.

When Albuquerque city councillors left town to see what makes a festival marketplace tick, when they hit the road to study singing fudge makers, did they go to Dubuque? When they conducted cost-benefit analyses on a cheese-making polka band, did they do it in Sheboygan? Did they go to Buffalo to see if Albuquerque was ready for taffy-pulling oboists? No. They went to Toledo, which has all these things, and which also is in Ohio.

Personally, I don't think we should stop at Toledo. I think Albuquerque should do everything humanly possible to become another Cleveland. Why should Cleveland be the only city in America to have a river that once was set on fire? Not too many years ago, the Cuyahoga was a fire hazard. Can you imagine the national recognition we'd get if we could pull a seven-alarm blaze on the Rio Grande? Think of the headline: "River Destroyed; Arsonist Sought."

And as long as I'm talking about civic pyromaniacs, a Cleveland mayor once dedicated a cement plant or a Baskins-Robbins store or something and while doing so was required to light an acetylene torch. So he did, and he set his hair on fire. Albuquerque needs a mayor like that.

Look at the Ohio financial world. The savings and loan business has been so good in Ohio that people have been lined up for blocks waiting to get in. Business was booming so much that the Ohio governor had to close seventy-one savings and loan associations so the employees could have a few days off to rest.

Do we have that kind of action around here? No way. We have the same old dull savings and loans. Walk in, stand in line, deposit money, choose toaster, walk out. There's not so much as a hint of the kind of excitement you get in Ohio where you never know if the Feds will charge in and shut down the savings and loan five minutes after you deposit every cent you have in the world.

And now, as if I need more proof that Ohio is a good role model, along comes something called The Road Information Program (TRIP), a Washington, D.C.-based organization representing industries that fill potholes. TRIP has released its annual pothole report. Guess who's the leader of the pack?

Ohio, naturally. TRIP says there are approximately 6,893,939 potholes in Ohio. The closest competition comes from Pennsylvania with 3,950,637. I called TRIP to verify this. A friendly young TRIP woman said every word was true.

"It's Ohio," she said. "Nobody comes close to topping Ohio."

How do you know? I asked. How do you figure how many potholes are in Ohio?

"We contacted state departments of transportation, found out how much tonnage of pothole filler they used and then figured how much it takes to fill a single pothole."

What about New Mexico? How did we do?

"Not too well, I'm afraid. New Mexico has approximately 309,000."

You're kidding. Ohio has 6,893,939 potholes and we've got a miserable 309,000?"

"That's the way it looks."

At first, this depressed me. I didn't see how we could make up that much ground. But then it occurred to me that TRIP's statistics measure only the number of potholes which have been filled. Having driven for years in New Mexico, I'll bet we have at least 6,893,939 potholes, just as many as Ohio, but we've gotten around to filling only 309,000. This a hopeful sign.

So I'm beginning to think we can close the gap between New Mexico and Ohio. It will be a challenge, but I think we're up to it. Now, if we can start working on incinerating that river . . .

10

Standing on the Edge

Robert Ruark is fifty-eight years old. He lives on an edge. He is polite and well spoken, as gracious a man as you will ever meet. But at the moment, he's living on this edge, this precipice; he maintains an uncomfortable balance, frightened by what he sees. He's never been here before.

He's not a bum. He's not a wino. But he sleeps with the bums and the winos, and eats with the bums and winos. He's come to know them well, and wants more than anything in the world not to become one of them.

Last year, his fencing business failed in Midland-Odessa, Texas. He worked for a while at a friend's office supply shop in Lubbock. Business slowed almost to a stop early this year. He moved on to Amarillo, where a temporary job led to another in Albuquerque. It melted away. He sleeps now at the Salvation Army, but can stay only a few days and then must leave to make room for others.

He has walked from downtown to Juan Tabo, looking for work. He's covered both sides of the street along Central. The next day he made the same trip along Lomas. No job. He asks for work, the only thing he's ever asked for in his life. No nickels and dimes. No handouts. There is no self-pity in his voice. Only wonder. Amazement at how he got to the edge.

"I've never drawn anything like food stamps or welfare . . . I mean . . . like these guys have checks coming in from everywhere," he says (the sound of his voice reflecting that he hasn't quite figured out how they do it).

"These guys on the bum, they know every little trick to

do things and get things. But all these things you learn. I never knew these things. You just don't think about them.

"Somebody comes along and asks you for a quarter, you give it to him just to get rid of him. Most people don't want to be around them. They're not clean. Some of them are a nuisance. And you want to know why they're a nuisance? Plain old loneliness. They're just plain lonely. They think if they can just get somebody to talk to . . . but they don't know anybody. Nobody will talk to them. So they become darn near recluse characters. Get up into a hide somewhere, up under a bridge, and they think, 'You know, if I can drink I'll forget about all these things . . . ' "

Drinking is an avenue not readily available for Robert Ruark. He says alcohol makes him sick, that he's never been able to drink, that he never liked going to work with a hangover.

His soft Texas accent is punctuated frequently by awe, almost reverence for what he sees as physiological impossibilities. "How can you sleep outside, drinking this cheap wine and not die?" he says. "I never knew the human body was so strong. A lot of these guys have been shot, stabbed, robbed . . . I'm just amazed at what the human body can stand."

The surprise is almost constant as he reflects on the wonder of it all, as he mulls over the reality that he could find himself, at the age of fifty-eight, standing at the edge, worried about soap and water.

"The problems I have basically are with keeping clean . . . keeping my clothes clean . . . protecting . . . I mean, you really get down to . . . Ordinarily, it's kind of automatic for most people. You do your laundry or whatever and . . . but it really becomes an important thing all of a sudden. The little things . . . just to survive . . . You're down to . . . I'm not sure where I'm going to put my clothes tonight."

There are other questions: Where are you going to sleep tonight? How are you going to get a sandwich? How are you going to get from Point A to Point B? And where are you going to get money, which is of particular interest to Robert Ruark. He's not any good at panhandling.

"I can't go and ask anyone for a quarter, but a lot of guys do this," he says, "and they've lost all self-respect, their pride and everything, you know. But at this point this is one of my big concerns."

Robert Ruark, who says he is the nephew of the late novelist of the same name, has thirty-two cents. The stream of disbelief flowing through his conversation continues unabated as he tries to figure out how it all came down to thirty-two cents.

"This is a shock to me. I guarantee you it's a heck of a shock. I can see why people steal. It's out of desperation. I saw a guy walk up to a cop and beg the cop to put him in jail. He said he didn't want to throw a rock through a window or anything. He said he was sick and hungry and wanted to go to jail. Can you imagine that? What an embarrassing thing to do."

When the disbelief temporarily recedes, he finds a pool of optimism. "I'll find something. I always have. I'm not gonna give up now," he says, pausing to laugh a short, ironic laugh. "I'm at the point where I'd almost do something for free just to have something to do. This is boring. I'll cut grass. I'll do dishes. Anything. I don't care what it is. I'm a good painter. I was thinking about going down and selling some blood, but I've never had to do that. I don't know if they'll take me at my age . . .

"But you gotta keep going. Everybody else is doing it. I guess I'll do it—except I'm not sure what it is I'm supposed to do."

11

Invasion of the Barrel Snatchers

Hollywood gave us Invasion of the Body Snatchers, *a chilling tale in which emotionless beings, spawned each night from oversized pea pods, took over the Earth. But what you are about to read, if you dare, is no movie script, no Hollywood press agent's babble. It is the true story of Albuquerque, a dying city, strangling under the Invasion of the Orange-and-White Street Barrels.*

It is hoped this message will find its way to the outside world before it is too late. Let it be known that what is written here is true, not a flight of fancy or the paranoid rantings of a lunatic. It is the story of a city writhing in nightmarish death throes. It is a horror movie come to life.

Albuquerqueans, sweltering in 102-degree heat, pick their way through the ravaged streets, oblivious to the danger, more worried about finding medfly fruit in their grocery stores than the orange-and-white menace all around them. Medflies are hardly the threat. What fly in his right mind would leave the Mediterranean for the Northeast Heights?

The danger is in the streets, spreading as we sleep. When we wake, there are more. They are everywhere. No quadrant is safe. Two months ago they appeared a block and a half from my home. I paid no attention. Soon they had disappeared; the newly paved street left no trace. Then, just weeks ago, a small hole appeared down the block. No workers were seen, just the hole and two Orange-and-White Barrels. The next morning there were still no workers, but now the Orange-and-White Barrels had grown to four. Like clothes hangers left in a seldom-used but fertile closet, the regeneration process was in full swing. Soon there would be more Orange-and-White Barrels than mayoral candidates.

At first, thinking the spread of the barrels was all in my imagination, I tried alternate routes to the office. It didn't work. I tried side streets where traffic was light (and street repairs out of the question). Detour begat detour, each marked by fifty or so Orange-and-White sentries. They were everywhere, sometimes for blocks and blocks. I tried the freeway. Orange-and-White Barrels stretched for miles, some sprouting blinking eyes. The march north had begun. Soon Santa Fe would fall.

This can't be happening, I thought. This isn't a movie. There must be an explanation. Hollywood's fiction haunted me as I dialed the phone. The hero in *Invasion of the Body Snatchers,* realizing the danger, had called the police, but the police had already been podded by the invaders. Little did I realize that life would imitate art so cruelly.

I called Street Maintenance and asked for a complete list of street projects. "What projects?" the innocent voice said, sending my stomach into a series of square knots.

"The ones all over the city," I said, trying to remain calm so as not to raise suspicion. I was transferred to another official in Street Maintenance. I asked for the list. "What projects?" he said. My heart sank. "Maybe you'd better call Engineering," he said.

A woman answered at Engineering and I asked for a list of street projects. "What projects?" she said. My pulse raced; the sweats began. "I think you should call Street Maintenance," she said.

It was over. They were winning. "I've talked to Street Maintenance," I countered. "They said, 'What projects?' and told me to call you." She put me on hold. Minutes later an engineer came on the line.

"They're not all street maintenance projects. A lot of them are water projects. It's a pretty good time to be in the street barrier business, though," he said, laughing heartily. His laughter did nothing to calm my fears. "Most of the work is done underground. Sometimes you have to let it sit for a day to see if another leak is going to show up. Some of those old steel lines are in pretty bad shape."

This probably will stand as the official explanation. Do not believe it. We have fought. The evidence is found each morning: Orange-and-White Barrels flattened, twisted, blasted to the side of the road, while the patriots and political prisoners rot in jail on trumped-up charges of DWI and reckless driving.

We cannot win. The weight of their numbers crushes us, forces us into detours and U-turns, always making us take the long way home, insuring that we are mad when we get there, screaming at the kids, kicking the dog, sloshing down gin and wondering when all this will end. We have become a city of sweaty, soaking-wet shirts stuck to the back of the driver's seat. We are held captive in a long, honking snarl of cars and trucks held firm under the flashing gaze of the Orange-and-White Barrel.

12

Merit Badges

Have you ever been embarrassed for someone? The embarrassment isn't yours; it's somebody else's, somebody you might not even know, but nonetheless you feel embarrassed for because he has done something so out of line that the result goes beyond funny and into embarrassing.

I'm feeling that way now, as I review some funny lines that will bring a smile or maybe a laugh to you but the more I look at them, the more embarrassing they become.

Albuquerque Girl Scout Troop 633 went to the Legislature last week. The girls were to be pages. After returning to Albuquerque, the scout leaders called to see if I would be interested in the girls' reactions to what they had seen.

Here is one fifth grader's response: "The people there were weird. They acted like first graders without a teacher in the room."

Girl Scout Troop 633 spent a year preparing for this trip. The girls were primed, excited, as well they should be. Did you ever visit the Legislature when you were in the fifth grade? Impressive, wasn't it? Remember that sense of awe, that feeling of having just walked into a holy place? Remember looking down at the vast semi-circular hall, listening to the booming oratory of senators and representatives? Very impressive.

The 1985 Legislature has been a little different, though, hasn't it? Most of us are aware of the difference. We've seen and heard it through the pens, microphones and cameras of reporters, broadcasters, editorial writers and political columnists. One columnist, who pretty much wrapped up the whole Legislature in a single sentence, asked if anyone could remember when such monumental pettiness and stupidity had been so equally divided between the two parties.

Well, here's how it looked through the eyes of Girl Scout Troop 633:

- "I learned that the first time you are a page you're confused, scared and nervous. I also learned that senators argue a lot and interrupt each other."
- "I thought it would be very strict, but while we were pages the senators started fighting and it was funny."
- "I learned that some people have a very short temper. I also learned that you can be quiet if you want to."
- "My day as a page was like being in a small kid's classroom. Before we got to Santa Fe and before I was a page, I thought everybody would be political and courteous, but it was exactly the opposite. The senators would ask somebody to read something and while that somebody was reading, everybody else would be talking to each other. It was very strange."
- "They were fighting like cats and dogs."
- "People didn't cooperate. They were laughing and acting like kids. They talked to their neighbors and didn't pay attention."
- "One senator said Will Rogers never met a man he didn't like. Another senator said Will Rogers never met Les Houston."
- "I think they could have acted more mature."
- "They'd introduce a bill and then talk about other things. Nothing got done."
- "They'd talk for half an hour and then vote, but they never talked about what they were voting on."
- "Sometimes they need to argue, but they need to argue about the right thing. They need to argue about what they're going to vote on."

A Girl Scout leader said one senator recognized the ludicrous picture being presented to the girls. The senator rose and chastised his colleagues for their behavior, saying that the legislators—*all* the legislators—had a duty to conduct themselves in a proper manner. He then spent another ten minutes saying that none of the blame lay on his side of the aisle, that the problems—*all* the problems—began on the other side of the aisle.

The day was not a total loss, though. A fourth grade Girl Scout, in one of those rare moments of stunning perceptiveness that seem to be the exclusive property of fourth graders, summed up the day this way. "I learned to help people who need help."

13
Walt

I'm not a cat person. I'm a dog person. I've been a dog person all my life. I have had many dogs, but only one cat, and I still have him. After 10 years, after several dogs have come and gone, I still have this cat, given to me as a Christmas present. I don't know why I still have this cat, but I've been thinking about it lately.

I started thinking about it just the other morning, a windy, cold—bitingly cold as a matter of fact—morning. Ever since that morning, when I climbed the extension ladder to retrieve him from the roof of my house, I have been thinking: *How is it that this cat has lasted with me for 10 years?*

There have been other times the question arose. There was the housesitting venture during which the cat found a way to get up between the ceiling and roof and stayed there for three days. There was the time I moved into a new house and thought, and maybe even prayed a little, that the cat had run away—until four days later when he came out from behind the refrigerator, looked around, and made it known that he hadn't eaten in four days.

There was the time we lived in the far North Valley and it was his custom to drag in lizard heads and stow them behind the living room sofa. There were the hundreds of times he hung from a screen door like a nervous mountain climber looking for a spare piton. I solved that by moving to a house with no screen door for him to hang from. Now, at 2 A.M. or so, he hurls himself at the glass-paned door until I let him in.

And I'm thinking: *What gives with this? Why would anybody put up with this?*

I'm not a cat person. I'm a dog person. But dogs come and go. Walter, the cat, stays. I don't even know any cat people. Everybody I meet says, "Well, I'm not really a cat person." Me, neither, I say—except for this one cat I've had for 10 years.

Dogs are cooperative; cats aren't. Dogs come when you call; cats don't. A dog person has no problem saying "Come!" and immediately a 102-pound German Shepherd, tail wagging, sits at your feet, begging to do something to make you even happier.

Cats come when they want to come. Cats go when they want to go. Besides, there's a world of difference between a grown man lowering his voice to say "Come!" and sticking his head out the door, cranking his larnyx into an unnatural, screechy falsetto and squeaking, "Here, kitty, kitty!"

The garbage bag in my house is in that storage area under the kitchen sink. The doors to that area are held shut with rubber bands, but it's not to keep the dog out. The dog doesn't open the doors and spread garbage around the house at 3 A.M. The cat does.

The dog inhales food, any food. The cat waits sometimes for hours, to see if anything better might come along.

The dog doesn't climb up on the roof, scream because she can't get back down, and then open my veins when I drag her off. The cat does.

The dog never, never jumps on my chest and uses my face as a foot rest, a *hind foot* foot rest. The cat does.

Walt is not a cute, cuddly cat. When I took him to the vet, the vet said, "Well, let's see how much this guy weighs." He lifted Walt, hesitated, and said, "Big cat."

A couple of guys in my poker game said, "That cat acts like a dog." I tell them I've always treated him like a dog, it's the only way I can live with him. But he's a cat.

I think I know now. I don't like admitting it, but I think I know. I'm jealous of him. I don't like him, but I'm jealous of him. And he knows it. I want to be like him, and I'm willing to put up with him in the hope I might learn how.

George Carlin said cats don't accept responsibility, that when they crash into a glass door, they act as if they *meant* to crash into the glass door. Stephen King, in *Pet Sematary,* said cats were the gangsters of the animal world, that they didn't live within the rules governing other animals. Cats made their own rules.

They're right. Walt is everything they say, and more, because Walt has lived longer than any cat has a right to. Walt has stayed around long enough to polish his basic cat obnoxiousness until it gleams.

My hope is that mixed in with all of Walt's dead hair, some of his character traits will rub off on me. It has to be a great way to live, and I'm wondering what life would be like if you could paw your nose at the world and the world's response would be, "Isn't that cute? Let's feed him again."

14

Is El Paso in Texas?

It's time we put this El Paso Water Grab to rest. We've argued, engaged in name-calling and other forms of uncivil behavior. It's time for compassion. I know that sounds strange coming from me, but this call for reason and humaneness is based on information from a trusted friend. And, yes, he's a Texan.

Simply stated, the Texans don't want El Paso, either.

I've never had any trouble understanding why New Mexicans don't want Texans around, much less Texans who steal our water. First, they buy up and brag up everything in sight and then, when somebody says he doesn't like it, the next thing you hear is some Texan whining because we all don't love him and he can't for the life of him figure out why.

So I have no trouble sympathizing with the New Mexican who called one day and said, "An oldtimer once told me that the way to solve the Texas water problem was to take up a collection, buy a few hundred miles of quarter-inch copper tubing—the kind you use on evaporative coolers—put one end in the Rio Grande and the other in Texas. If the SOBs can suck as hard as they blow, they'll have all the water they need."

At one time I contemplated equally drastic measures. I thought we might ask White Sands to give the range the day off, turn the missiles around and nuke El Paso. But it would have been one more waste of government time and money. If you've been to El Paso, you know what it looks like, so you also know we could nuke it and when the smoke cleared, we wouldn't be able to tell if we had hit it.

These radical propositions came about because El Paso

wants to drill 266 wells and take out 246,000 acre-feet of water per year, or about 80 billion New Mexican gallons. This prospect gets New Mexicans to thinking about closing borders, nuking cities and buying hundreds of miles of copper tubing.

But I've changed my mind. I got to thinking about a conversation I had years ago and that memory has caused me to ease up a little on El Paso. My first newspaper job was in Las Cruces. When I arrived, I called my old buddy, Gary the Texan. I told him I was getting closer to Texas. He asked where I was and I said about 40 miles from El Paso. There was a long silence before he spoke again.

"I don't know where this El Paso is," he said, "but it's not in Texas."

Of course it is, I said. Look at the map.

"Oh, all right," he said, sort of grudgingly. "I suppose you're technically right, but we don't claim it."

When I got to thinking about that conversation, I decided to call him for some elaboration. After listening to me explain the hard feelings generated by the El Paso Water Grab, he said none of it surprised him.

"It's about what I'd expect from them," he said. "I suppose we're going to have border wars, aren't we?"

Please remember this man is Texan to the core. He was born and reared in El Campo; his sister lives in Austin; his momma lives outside Kirbyville. They all talk funny, especially his sister, whom he admits is unintelligible. He now lives in Beaumont, which is not the crown jewel of Texas. An hour in downtown Beaumont heightens your appreciation of Love Canal. In spite of his impeccable Texas credentials, however, he maintains an aversion to El Paso.

"To be honest," he said, "we've been hoping for some sort of natural disaster. You know, an earthquake or something that would change the course of the Rio Grande and permanently put El Paso in Mexico."

I pressed for further explanation of his adamant disassociation from the Texas border city.

"Well, it's not that I hate it or anything. Just a few weeks ago I was on my way to Arizona and I flew over it. By the way, I suppose you should know that the pilot said if we looked out the window, we could see the El Paso River."

The what?

"I thought you'd like that. Well . . . Oh, I don't know . . . look, it's already bad enough that when most people think of Texas, they think of Dallas. Dallas is just where people from Houston go to buy western wear. El Paso is . . . well, it's where we go when we want to go to Mexico. It's just not part of our consciousness. In my part of Texas we have Louisiana to contend with. I know El Paso has a water problem, but so do we. We don't know where to put it all."

I was still groping for a satisfactory explanation of this ideological split when he said something that made New Mexico's uphill battle quite clear. It came as I was explaining the court cases evolving from the water grab. He said it matter-of-factly, without a hint of the usual loudmouth, Texas bragging. In fact, he said it so simply, so calmly, that it froze the blood in my veins.

"You may not have a case," he said. "The Rio Grande belongs to us. Everybody knows that."

15

To Calendarize

Whenever my old buddy Gary the Texan is in town, certain rituals are maintained. I have to remind him that it's not nice to steal other people's water and he has to remind me that El Paso isn't in Texas, so he has nothing to say about water stealers; and then I have to show him the map and he has to say that whoever made the map wasn't a Texan, because no Texan would admit that El Paso is anywhere near the state.

Gary the Texan has been at his small university for many years, though he's studiously (if you'll pardon the phrase) avoided holding down a job there. He's always managed to dodge a contract by living "hand to grant"; but now he's close to signing a contract, close to becoming a full-fledged, full-time employee, and that means attending official staff meetings. He's been to a couple and he's concerned that he's the only person in the room who gags when somebody says the meeting was called "to calendarize the school for the next semester."

"That's *calendarize*," Gary says, "from the verb 'to calendar, from a great height.'"

We talked about his university's open admissions policy. "Open admissions is a tragedy," he says. "We tell them they don't have to read in order to get into college, but we don't tell them they have to read in order to stay there."

Gary teaches reading to college students, not so they can teach it to first graders, but so they can learn to read themselves. Each class meeting he has them bring in any words they came across and didn't understand since the last meeting of the class. One brought in the word *comprehensive*. The student said the school had been giving him comprehensive tests since September but he didn't know what *comprehensive* meant.

"Another one brought in the word *fornication*," Gary says. "She said she heard it in her church. It was used in a sermon by the minister. I asked if the minister was for it or against it. She said she didn't know because she didn't know what the word meant. I told her what it meant. She said, 'Oh.' "

I told Gary I couldn't imagine myself doing what he does. I said I didn't think I had the patience or perseverence.

"You could do it if you saw them," he says. "These kids have been cheated. They have a right to their language. They're not stupid. But they've been cheated. I've got to get them to trust me enough to tell me what they don't know, because they know what they're supposed to know and they're not likely to admit that they don't know it. That's how they got through high school.

"They sat in the back of the classroom and didn't make any trouble. I had one come in who was wearing a high school graduation ring the size of a door knob. He was amazed that those symbols on the paper actually stood for something. He had about a third grade reading level."

"Educationists" would be uncomfortable in the company of this Texan. They'd be thrown off balance because he's on the side of the kids, and he's got a few ideas about why the kids aren't learning.

"I went to observe a student teacher," Gary says. "She had been given to me by another professor in the middle of the semester. She was teaching the third grade. It was in an old school and it was an overcast and rainy morning. I just knew it was going to be a bad day at Black Rock.

"The kids were sitting quietly at their desks and the first thing the student teacher shouted was, 'Get quiet!' I cringed but didn't say anything. She was doing it to show me she had discipline in her classroom. Well, she was wearing wooden-soled shoes, and it was an old wooden floor. All morning it was Clomp! Clomp! Get quiet!... Clomp! Clomp! Get quiet! . . . You could call it the Student Teacher Two-Step. But she was the only one making noise. I was getting madder and madder. Pretty soon the kids were giving her looks like they were getting ready to throw her through the window. I got up and left, because I knew if they did, I'd join them.

"When I talked to her later and suggested that she might wear soft-soled shoes, she looked at me as if I were insane. I know she left that room and told the first person she saw that she had talked to a crazy man. But she's the reason kids aren't going to learn anything."

It remains to be seen if my Texan friend will sign a contract, but even if he does, it's doubtful he will begin "calendarizing" his semesters. He'll likely continue to make comments like the one he made on the evaluation sheet of a special education student teacher. After observing a disastrous day in the classroom, he entered a single remark on the entire evaluation.

Under the Good Points section he wrote, "Nobody was killed."

16
House Safari

I have been hunting for a house. I'm relaxed about it now, a veteran, nothing like the gape-jawed rookie I was a few weeks ago. I thought it would be a worthwhile public service to pass along my *Ten Rules for Happy House Hunting*.

1. Do not let the condition or price of a house disturb you. You will quickly get over the shock of seeing astronomically priced houses that could have been built only by Landfill Estates or one of its subsidiaries. The owners of these houses are not being outrageous in their pricing. They are merely taking the old saw: *A Man's Home Is His Castle,* and adding a capitalistic corollary: *A Home Doesn't Have to Be a Castle in order to Cost as Much as One.*

2. Sit back and enjoy the ride as you and your real estate agent drive around town in search of keys. (Generally, most real estate agents drive huge cars—Caddies, Lincolns, and the like. Before you sign up with a realtor, be sure to ask. No one wants to drive around town in a Chevy Vega while looking for keys.) Keys have a way of moving from person to person and are never where you were told they would be. During these key-searching forays you will become more familiar with real estate offices than you ever imagined. Take note of these buildings as they are leading economic indicators. For instance, one well-appointed Northeast Heights office has masking tape holding up the letters on the front of its building. This gives the viewer a greater appreciation for the debilitating effects of rising interest rates, and if the real estate office can't afford to fix two lousy letters, you can

imagine what the bank is going to do to you when it comes time to set your interest rate.

3. Be aware of the differences between making appointments with sellers who live in the house and renters who live in the house being sold. Sellers generally say, "Sure, come on over, anytime." Tenants, not in any hurry to tenant someplace else, generally ask for specific times: "If you can't be here between 7:15 and 7:17, I just can't make it."

4. Do not be taken aback when you enter a house and something at your feet grabs you by the collar, yanks your head down and screams, "I'M THE BURNT ORANGE CARPET WITH RED TRIM! LOOK AT ME!" Along the same lines, be prepared for the ROYAL PURPLE! or WILTED-LETTUCE GREEN! carpet in the bedrooms. You will not find any home to be perfect, but on the other hand, take a minute to think what it will be like first thing in the morning—every morning—when you walk into your PHOSPHORESCENT APRICOT! bathroom.

Also, in the matter of baths, half-baths means no bath, unless your parakeet is going to use the sink.

5. Be prepared for the "followers." There are homeowners who say, "Just walk around. Take your time. If you have any questions, I'll be in the living room," which is true only as long as *you* are in the living room. When you go to another room, the owner is at your heels, like a department store detective who thinks you have the look of a pantyhose thief.

6. Be prepared for a wave of inadequacy when viewing retired couples' homes. The gardens are exquisite; the lawns well tended and closely cut. These areas are beautiful and you must have enough courage to admit that they won't be for long after you move in.

7. When you find *the* house, don't be dispirited when you walk into the back yard and look up at the second-story apartment dwellers next door who are looking down at you.

Should you find *the* house with no apartments in the neighborhood, be sure you stand in front, look up and down the block at the meticulously cared-for homes. Take special note of one house that looks like it barely survived the Dresden fire bombing. It will be in a woeful state of disrepair. In front will be three cars, all in various stages of cannibalization. Should you have trouble spotting this house, here is a helpful hint: It's right next to the one you want.

8. In many back yards you will find true natural landscaping, which is to say, landscaping untouched by human hands, which is to say, no landscaping. While nodding appreciatively, agree with the owner when he says. "This is the perfect place for a pool."

9. Many older homes have been remodeled by the owners. Your experiences in these homes will heighten your powers of diplomacy to a level comparable to the U.S. State Department. Should you see the new master bedroom, the one with a cathedral archway entrance, you won't even think of asking when the pope slept there. Always be polite and sincere when you say, "Lovely bedroom. You've done some nice work there. I especially like the mirrored tile on the walls and the ceiling. It's subtle, but makes a statement."

10. Don't give up. It's out there somewhere. You'll find it.

17

Stupid Name for a Dog

Want to hear from your friends? Want to hear from people you've never heard of in your life? Want to have these people open vaults of trivia and make large deposits in your ears? While drinking your first cup of coffee in the morning, would you be interested in being publicly humiliated by . . . a newspaper photographer?

Nothing to it. All you have to do is mistake Buster Brown's flea-bitten, raggedy dog for a box of soap.

This past Friday morning, in this space generally devoted to high-minded discussions and literary excursions of wide renown, I called Tige Tide.

"Tide!" the photographer said, sipping his coffee and looking at the column in his Friday's paper.

Yeah. Tide.

"That's soap, you dope. It's not Tide. It's Tige."

Tige?

"Tige. Short for Tiger."

Are you sure?

"Want to bet ten bucks?"

You're that sure?

"I'm not sure of many things, but I'm sure of this. You're going to hear from people on this one."

Well, now he can be sure of two things: the dog's name is indeed Tige, and there is an abnormally large number of people in this town who enjoy it when they get a chance to point out just how stupid some of my stupid mistakes are.

Write something ungrammatical and people write to let you know that the weakness of your argument is exceeded only by the weakness of your English grammar education. I have such a letter in front of me now: "Me write to inquire whom in hell edits your copy. I have been lying in wait for you for quite awhile."

I know about these people; I know they've been out there for a long time, lurking, patiently waiting, like a mob of retired English teachers in a duck blind. I read of the columnist who said, "When I started writing this column, I didn't know there would be three million English teachers out there." It's true; they're out there. Misplace a comma and they write.

But when it comes to Tide, people don't write. Tide is too good, too juicy to let sit around for the time it would take to write a letter. Tide can't be trusted to the postal service.

"Normajean, let the bacon burn. Come in here and look at what this moron has done. He's called a dog a box of soap." This calls for action, telephonic action.

All day the phone rang. All day I listened.

"Was Buster Brown's dog all-temperature?"

"At least Tide was clean enough to be in the restaurant with you."

Oh, aren't we having fun today?

Why do I have so much trouble with dogs? I'm kind to dogs. I spent my GI years in K-9 units. Now that I think of it, that was probably where the trouble began. I should have known that first day of training when the instructor read the list and assigned each of us a dog. I should have known the karma was bad or something when that master sergeant called out my name and assigned a dog named Rin-Tin-Tin to me.

"Arnholz, 5792-Rinty."

What? What did you say? Rinty? *Rin-ty?* As in Rin-Tin-Tin?

"5792-Rinty."

Oh, God . . .

Just a few months ago, I wrote what I thought was a perfectly innocent remark about pit bulls. I forgot pit bulls get bad press, and pit bull people are sensitive. I had to write another column apologizing to pit bulls. I don't even know if they read it. It'll probably turn out that Tide, or Tige, or whatever that miserable dog's name is, was a pit bull.

Tide dies hard. I don't want to let go of Tide. I have believed all my life that Buster Brown's dog was named Tide. Hi, my name's Buster Brown and I live in a shoe. That's my dog, Tide, and he lives in there, too.

These people had to be wrong. I took a walk downtown to think it over. When I returned, my desk had been transformed into a floral arrangement of bright pink phone messages.

"When Buster washed Tide, did he use cold water so Tide's coat wouldn't shrink?"

"How much will they charge me if I bring my soap to a spay/neuter clinic?"

"Was Tide purebred or low suds?"

"Which Tide? Ebb?" (There's always a strange one.)

"My laundromat has a sign in the front window that says 'No Pets.'"

All right, all right, never again will I mention Buster Brown or *Tige* . . . *Tige* . . . *Tige* . . . Stupid name for a dog.

18

I Went Flying with Him One Day

Dennis Young died about a year ago. I just found out about it. I hardly knew him. He wasn't a friend or even a casual acquaintance. All I did was go flying with him one day.

He was an Air Force helicopter pilot; he flew an H-53 Super Jolly Green Giant (that's an Air Force designation for several tons of metal that have no business leaving the ground).

That brief meeting comes back to me now. I remember little details about him. I was doing a story on the 1550th Aircrew Training and Test Wing at Kirtland Air Force Base. And one day I flew with Dennis Young.

There have been other times when I've met people briefly, only to hear later that they had died. I would say, "That's too bad," and then not think about it much. But that's not the case with this pilot. I wouldn't doubt that Dennis Young forgot my name as soon as we landed, but there was something about flying with this helicopter pilot, something about putting my safety in the hands of a polite young man, Air Force-polite, by the book, yes-sir-no-sir polite, that makes me remember.

He was all professional, all check list, no fooling around, chit-chat held to a minimum—until we flew to the Melrose gunnery range. When we neared the range, Dennis Young contacted the Melrose tower for clearance to enter the area. There was a moment of silence before the controller in the tower came on and said the range was closed for maintenance. A few more silent seconds passed. Dennis Young asked the tower to repeat the message. It was repeated.

In the rear of the helicopter his crew and a para-rescue

instructor laughed it up, some of them pointing at my note-book and mouthing the words "Write that down! Write that down!"

I looked toward the cockpit. Dennis Young, not wanting to believe this was happening on the day he took a reporter for a ride, sat at the controls, his head slowly shaking from side to side. Then his voice came across the headset. It would be the only time there were no yes sirs or no sirs or technical data or explanations of the mission. It would be a simple, straightforward statement: "Somebody has skeeee-rooood up!"

Now he's dead. He was on an air-to-air refueling mission off the coast of Okinawa when the helicopter rotor struck the fuel line trailing behind a lumbering C-130 tanker. The helicopter went down in the Pacific.

Dennis Young kept airborne for about 10 minutes. He headed for the nearest landfall. He had to. Some helicopters will float; H-53s sink. He was about a minute from a small island when it happened.

It had never happened that way before; the Air Force didn't know it could. The tail section of the helicopter, damaged in some way, snapped off. The H-53 went down and sank with Dennis Young and his crew still strapped in their seats.

A pilot I talked to said it was likely that the tail section was vibrating badly, but the severity of the vibrations could not be felt in the forward part of the aircraft. As he spoke, I thought of the day we hovered over the Sandias; I remembered the shuddering of that enormous piece of metal as Dennis Young, bucking a heavy wind, held the helicopter steady while a para-rescueman was lowered on a hoist to the ground. All check list. No fooling around. Dennis Young was probably check-listing his way to that island when his craft fell apart. Check-listing along, trying to figure out a way to keep the thing flying.

Those flights are strong and clear in my mind. I'm still not sure why. Maybe it's that little boy fascination with the big flying machine, the scarf flapping in the wind, the pilot's monotone, "Y'all don't worry about that li'l 'ol red light on the instrument panel." Maybe it's that recognition that life is fragile, but I'm still going to fly my machine and thumb my nose at the fragility.

Those flights stay with me, but why, I don't know for sure. I do know that a bond is formed up there. No matter how brief the time, a union is made. It sets you apart. It's the reason flyers walk and talk a little differently; there's something about them that sets them apart from those stuck on the ground. There's a difference between them and us, and the difference is that any way you cut it, they're up there and we're down here.

I hardly knew Dennis Young. Never went drinking with him. Never met his wife; as a matter of fact, I don't even know if he was married. I just went flying with him one day.

19

Is It Winter Yet?

If you look at a perfectly good overcast, ominous, cold, slate gray (would-be novelists will immediately recognize the always-dependable "slate gray") sky, and all you see is an overcast, ominous, cold, slate gray sky, you have permission to stay at home—with the drapes closed—and sulk.

Monday morning started out as a peach of a day. You could see your breath as you walked out the door. You shivered and the car shivered under a breathtakingly leafless tree. It had all the makings of a nice winter day. And what happens, first thing, at work? Somebody complains.

"I sure would like to see the sun one of these days," somebody says.

I keep my mouth shut, but it isn't easy, because I'm one of the few people I know who doesn't complain about cold weather when it's cold. I don't wait for summer to say, "Boy, I wish it would cool off." I don't wait for winter to say, "Boy, I wish it would warm up." No matter what time of year, I'm always willing to stick up for winter.

Consider the advantages of winter. Think back to July, when it was 104 degrees. Did you curl up with your sweetheart in front of the swamp cooler and sip cold buttered rums? Of course you didn't. You know exactly what you did. You didn't move. It was too hot. You probably yelled at your sweetheart because she told you the best she could do was fix room-temperature toddies.

Remember getting into your car and not beng able to touch the steering wheel because you thought you were grabbing a Tularosa Basin branding iron? That doesn't happen in the winter, does it? You can hop right in and grab the steering wheel; you have no worries about how searingly hot it will be, leaving you free to pound it with your fist or viciously turn it back and forth because the cold has sucked the life from your battery and the car won't start. But at least you don't sweat heavily.

You get to know your neighbors in the winter. You even get to know strangers (a term often interchangeable with "neighbors") in the winter. You learn to say "Do you have jumper cables?" with just as much cheery warmth and good-heartedness as "Merry Christmas!" In the summer, all you can do is sit by the roadside as the steam rises from under the hood of the car.

Just a moment ago, I passed by the desk of a reporter who was talking on the phone. "Well, they've got snow in Bernalillo," he said. There was no joy in his voice, which in one sense is good, because reporters are supposed to be objective. But I don't think objectivity had anything to do with it.

"Snow in Bernalillo" is cause for rejoicing. "Snow in Bernalillo" virtually guarantees that no one in Bernalillo will spend the day with a wet, sticky shirt plastered on his back. "Snow in Bernalillo" means that, with a little luck, it will soon be "Snow in Albuquerque."

Don't people realize what that means? Fewer traffic jams, for one thing. Just a forecast of snow is enough to keep half the drivers in Albuquerque off the streets. And, if there is a traffic jam, it won't feel like a traffic jam, because it's not hot.

When it's 104, you'll hear someone say, "It's miserable out there." When it's 24 and the wind chill factor makes it 13 below, you'll hear, "It's miserable out there." But listen to the different tones of voice; 24 is a lot easier to handle than 104. You can do something about 24 or 13 below. You can put on a sweater or hold hands in front of the fire or go outside and chop wood. Chop long enough and pretty soon you don't notice how cold it is. Try chopping wood when it's 104 and see how you feel.

I don't understand people who complain about winter. When

it snows, don't kids run outside and holler, "Hooray! It's snowing!" Don't Mom and Dad run to the living room window to watch the snow gracefully float down from the heavens? Have you ever heard anybody running to the window like that in the summer. Have you ever heard kids squealing, "Hooray! It's 104!" Have you ever seen Mom and Dad rush to the living room window to watch the heat waves floating gracefully up to the heavens?

The proper approach to winter lies in the proper attitude toward winter. If you look up at that overcast, ominous, cold, slate gray sky, and that's all you see, then that's all you get. The trick is to look at the overcast, ominous, cold, slate gray sky and remember that inside every cloud is a steaming bowl of posole.

20
Slugs

Three-day weekends were made for slugs, but only if the slug maintains the proper pace. Interrupt that pace and the slug is in trouble. For instance, the three-day weekend just past began when an old and dear friend called to say, "You slug!"

The epithet was hurled only because I had written a column pointing out the merits of card playing as excellent exercise (burns up more than 1.9 calories a minute). In that same column, I also pointed out that sitting quietly and standing quietly were other beneficial exercises.

"You slug!" she said again, before inviting me to join her and her husband for a mountain hike, a long mountain hike, a hike from Sandia Crest to Placitas, an 11-mile trek over rocks, around and through bushes, and all on a day when the temperature was forecast to be in the high 90s.

I declined, was again called a slug, ignored this repeated cruelty, and offered to pick up the hikers at the end of the trail and drive them back to their car at the Crest. Wasn't that nice of me? Especially when you consider I had no idea that just three-quarters of a mile away from the trail a cattle guard would destroy my car's muffler?

You meet the nicest people while enjoying the great outdoors. I mean, there it was, a fine summer day, 99 degrees, my car was hung up on a cattle guard, the muffler twisted and dangling, clanking between two steel rails in the cattle guard, and me, hot, sweaty and saying things I can't say here. Then along comes a man—a big man, the sort of mountain man you might see in a Grape Nuts commercial. I asked him if I could borrow a hacksaw, the hacksaw being the only way I saw of removing the deceased muffler.

"I'll get my tools," he said. "If you cut it off, you'll have to buy a new one and they'll just charge you an arm and a leg."

He returned with tools and a log about two feet long and eight inches thick. He put the tools on the ground, handed me the log, turned his back to the car, did a deep knee bend, grabbed ahold of the undercarriage of the car, and said, "I'll lift her up and you put the log under her."

OK.

He lifted, the car came up, I put the log under, and said something about how it was certainly more efficient than a jack.

He said, "I change my tires this way all the time."

Getting the muffler off was a struggle but we did it and crammed it into the back seat. After thanking him profusely, I drove on, now operating a mufflerless Volkswagen Rabbit that sounded more like an armored personnel carrier.

The hikers showed up soon after I arrived. Both were exhausted. They had run out of water and one was close to dehydration. Their small dog was in considerably worse shape and had to be carried the last two miles or so. One hiker said that about halfway down the mountain he followed through on an urge to scream, "This is the last 11-mile hike I ever go on!" (I let this pass without comment, although there is no vindication as sweet as that of the vindicated slug.)

The drive up to Sandia Crest and back to the city was without incident, except for the excruciatingly slow-moving carload of Oklahoma tourists in front of us. I imagine that when they return to Altus or Tulsa or wherever, the story will be told many times about the mountain road madman who went careering around them in a brown Volkswagen Rabbit that sounded like an armored personnel carrier.

Back at the hikers' house, we continued the three-day weekend the way three-day weekends were meant to be: We poured something cool to drink and sat at a small, shaded back yard table. It would have been perfect if I hadn't knocked my glasses off the table and shattered a lens.

I figure I burned up a good three or four calories leaning over to pick them up. Then there was the drive to Texas Optical and the walk from the parking lot . . . by the end of the day, I was beat.

21

That's a Relief

How do I start this? How do I put it delicately enough to . . . Ahem . . . I have before me a magazine article on how the driver of a car moving at seventy miles an hour may relieve himself of consumed coffee through the normal bodily function for such things and not lose so much as one mile an hour. What you do is crack open the door, lean over and . . . lean over and . . . well, you know.

Right from the start I should comfort you with the knowl edge that this practice is suggested and described in great detail by a Texan—and better than that, he's doing it on Texas highways. I bring it to your attention only because he may cross the state line one day and you should know what to look for.

His name is Gordon Baxter. He writes for one of those automotive magazines that seem to have a long shelf life in laundromats—which just happens to be the only place I read these automotive magazines, mostly because I haven't been seventeen for a long time (which is when most males stop reading automotive magazines).

Anyway, I was in the laundromat when I started reading about Gordon's trips to Dallas. It's a long haul, about five hours at seventy miles an hour. Gordon figures it takes five hours if he doesn't stop to eat and if he carries a thermos of one-hundred-mile coffee. Naturally, the coffee is great for staying awake, but it creates a problem, the problem being that Gordon has to figure out if he's going to drive through the pain or make a stop that will demolish his speed average—which is something to worry about if you're older than seventeen and still reading these magazines. (Driving more than fifty-five miles an hour is something of an obsession for the boys at this car magazine. Gordon's treatise is only one of three in defense of every American's right to a lead foot.)

Gordon says that at seventy miles an hour, there is sufficient slipstream around a slightly opened car door to create a powerful low-pressure area. Right away, he warns everybody to make sure you've got enough freedom of movement, so when you lower your lower garments, lower them so they're hanging down around your knees; he says you shouldn't go farther than your knees because that hogties your ankles, and your feet should be apart, too. He also says that serious concentration is vital to this operation, and I, for one, see no reason to question him on that point.

Is everybody following this? We are now traveling seventy miles an hour, our pants are down around our knees and we are concentrating like hell.

OK, next thing you do is unfasten your seat belt, so you can roll your body to the left. Gordon says you should try this in light traffic, because if you're new at the game you might swerve or veer a little at first.

Everybody still there? We are now traveling seventy miles an hour with our pants down and our seat belts off. We are concentrating. Novices swerve, although Gordon doesn't make it clear exactly how. At any rate, should you see a car with Texas license plates, and the driver's door is cracked open, and the driver is sort of rolled to the left and leaning out just a little bit and . . . Forewarned is forearmed. We continue with the lesson.

Theoretically, all you have to do now is keep your eye on the road, because the partial vacuum and centered wind pressures will take care of . . . everything else. Remember that safety counts. We are keeping our eyes on the road, reasonably sure at this point that the lesson is directed at those of the male persuasion and never will be reprinted in *Ms*.

We now come to the most crucial part of the entire lesson. It is impossible to sufficiently stress its importance.

Don't tailgate, so you won't have to stop all of a sudden.

A sudden stop might cause the door to swing forward and cause . . . Gordon says it will cause eddies and burbles in the slipstream and the effect will be reversed.

At this point, we've got to be honest enough to admit that there are times when we might wish an occasional wayward eddy and burble upon a fellow who drives down the road at seventy miles an hour with his pants down around his knees while hanging out the door.

However, Gordon's admonition that we not tailgate is well-taken, especially if we are driving behind Gordon. Should you spot a suspicious car bearing the black and white license plates of our neighbor to the east, it would behoove you to keep a safe distance. Beyond the obvious safety factor, you must keep in mind that eddies are not particularly discriminating about where they burble.

If you think you want to try this thing, have at it, but if you have the bad luck of falling out of your car at seventy miles an hour with your pants down around your knees (not your ankles, remember), and should you have the good luck of surviving, do yourself a favor and have enough presence of mind not to burble out some silly explanation.

22

Attention: Students

Education has got to be the fattest target. Everybody shoots at it, and everybody thinks they hit it. Picking on teachers and schools is a snap, so what you want to do is take it easy, give education a break. You want to tell people who complain that it isn't easy to control a room full of kids, much less teach them while you're at it. You want to tell people that sometimes it isn't the greatest job and the pay stinks, too. That's what you want to tell people.

Then along comes something such as . . . well . . . such as the *1981–82 Albuquerque High School Student Handbook.* That handbook is going to add a few pounds to that already overweight, fat target.

You must give the benefit of doubt on typos. Typos can happen to anybody. You must disregard "judgement," "dicipline," "transcrips," "soluation," "deptheria," and "chemestry."

But there are other offerings:

• *Our athletic colors are green and white with gold as a color used to denote our academic color combination.* If the football plays are that complicated, the Bulldogs are in big trouble.

• *The Board of Education has specified the least number of requirements in order to provide to each student the maximum latitude in selecting the program best suited to the career goal of each.* Maximizing latitudes at the education/career choice interface should be accomplished with a minimum of longitudinal interference with cross-reference to polysyllabic communicators addressing green and white with gold communicatees. We hope the kids get jobs, too.

• *AHS assures parents that any trips sponsored by the*

school are carefully supervised. By faculty. This is reassuring to parents and should comfort them. By gum.

- *The educational plan of some students includes college training. Although the specifics will vary with each student and each college.* You should be aware of this if you plan on attending college, where you might be required to write a complete sentence. Although the college probably will let you in anyway.

- *A student who owes any other school should clear with that school before registering at Albuquerque High School.* If you don't pay what you owe, we'll put a lien on your Camaro.

- *. . . staying in an orderly line and maintaining as quiet a noise level as possible.* Stay in line and don't talk.

- NOTE TO PARENTS: *Arrange for prompt and regular attendance and comply with attendance rules and procedures.* If you are going to be late for class or miss class, obtain explanatory note from your boss or child.

- *Attendance is taken and reported by IBM cards every period of the day."* If you have missed roll call, report to your IBM card in the tiniest office you've ever seen. IBM cards will have regular hours.

- *If a student is absent from school the parent must send a note upon the students return to school. The note should include parents signature, the date or dates of absences, and the reason for the absences. The note will be given to the students homeroom teacher by the student and will become a part of the students attendance file.* Under no circumstances will the note contain a single apostrophe denoting the possessive.

- *School starts at 8:00 A.M. to 3:00 P.M.* Come in when you can make it.

- *1. There are no blanket fees charged at AHS.*
  2. There are, at various times, project charges made . . .
  3. 2nd I.D. cost is $1.00.

These are reasonable rules—except all three are preceded

by this: *Two statements need to be made about fees.* Oh, well, everybody hates math.

These examples—and there are more—increase crankiness in parents. Parents might want to throw cream pies, or maybe rocks when they get to the back of the handbook and read "13 Lucky Ways To Improve Your Test Scores."

They might reach for the biggest rock available when considering that luck doesn't have anything to do with improving a test score. Work does. Knowledge isn't a blackjack game. You don't cut the cards and say, "I'll take a B minus."

The advice given in 13 Lucky Ways is good. It talks of good eating habits, a good night's rest, confidence, listening carefully to directions. Though they have nothing to do with luck, the 13 Lucky Ways are not to be ignored—especially No. 13: *Edit, check and proofread your answers.*

That's good advice for taking a test, or writing a handbook.

23

Disappointing the Duke

It didn't work out the way I always thought it would. It didn't work out the way it does in daydreams, where emergencies are met with decisive action and courage, and usually a little violence to whatever representative of urban villainy happens to confront you.

It just didn't work out that way. Friends said I did the sensible thing. Maybe. But it sure won't get me any work in Marlboro ads.

I had finished lunch and was walking along Central Avenue when he appeared. I don't know where he came from, one of the storefront doorways I guess. He planted himself in front of me, his face about six inches from mine. "Me and you are gonna discuss your financial situation," he said.

From the way he said this, I was pretty sure he was interested in the betterment of his and the decline of mine. He was not the typical panhandler; I'm accustomed to those. This guy was aggressive; he didn't have to tell me that if the discussion wasn't a good one, I'd be in trouble. My guess is that he once was an even-tempered, mild-mannered panhandler who one day asked for a quarter, but instead was given one of those assertiveness books, which he not only read but took to heart. And now our meeting was the result.

He had been drinking, but wasn't falling down drunk, not even staggering. My first thought was OK, *what's it going to be, Jim? An inside right. He'll never know what hit him. Maybe a lightning kick to the groin and then an agonizing arm lock until a downtown cop comes clopping by on a horse and cuffs the creep.* That's what I thought about, along with all the times I was going to get in shape and sign up for a karate class, but went to a movie instead.

Then I noticed he had one hand in his coat pocket. Was he armed? Did he have a gun? A knife? What if I didn't put him out of commission with one blow? Suddenly a newspaper headline popped into my mind: "Assertive Panhandler Drills Columnist on Central Avenue in Broad Daylight."

He wanted to discuss financial situations. I thought maybe a quick retort, some indication that I was no one to be messed with would throw him off, make him think twice before he tried to put the arm on me.

"Oh yeah," I said.

That was it. That was the quick retort designed to put the fear of God in this creep. Nothing else came out. Only "Oh, yeah." It wasn't exactly what I had in mind, but there it was.

Not unexpectedly, he said, "Yeah," finishing his reply with, "Cuz my financial situation's real bad."

I was trying to find another good comeback when he looked slowly to his left, toward the street. I looked in the same direction. A motorist was preparing to get into his car and apparently had seen what was going on. He stood by his car and watched. I had an ally.

My assertive friend turned back to me. "We'll talk about this in a minute," he said.

I was going to say "Oh, yeah" again, but I remembered I had already tried it and it hadn't worked out so well.

But I did know this was my chance. He wasn't paying attention to me, though his hand was still menancingly jammed into his coat pocket. I stepped back carefully. He continued to watch my ally who continued to watch from the curbside. I was now far enough away to get some real force into a punch.

For some reason, though, I looked toward the street. It was in its usual midday form, which is to say traffic was hardly moving. I quickly asked a blessing on the mayor and his angle parking policy that makes it possible to take three days to drive from First Street to Seventh (if you hit all the green lights). Then I stepped into the street, weaving my way through the cars until I reached the sidewalk on the other side.

I looked back and saw my ally getting into his car. The assertive panhandler with the weak financial statement continued down the sidewalk, presumably to look for someone else to consult with.

I went into a dress shop and called the police. I told them I would wait in the dress shop, as I was sure I could identify this guy. I waited for about ten minutes, but no one showed up, proving that this sort of thing doesn't get much priority—unless you're a participant.

Back at the office, everyone I talked to said I did the sensible thing. Still, it bothers me. As an American male I have bred into me a certain loyalty to the memory of John Wayne and I felt I had failed, but at least I'm ready for the next time. I've got the experience now.

It's a matter of being alert, of knowing how to recognize the instant when the advantage is yours. I know what to look for now.

I just hope the traffic's jammed up so I can make it across the street again.

24

The Wind Mussed His Hair

Today I saw Pete V. Domenici, United States senator from New Mexico and chairman of the Senate Budget Committee. He's had his picture and his words in *Time* and *Newsweek*, he's been on television coast-to-coast. Today I saw him walking down the sidewalk in the bright sunshine. The wind mussed his hair.

I didn't talk to him. I didn't interview him or run up and say, "Senator, will you comment on . . ." I only watched him walk down Gold Street and thought about all the photos and videotapes I had seen of important government officials in other countries—especially the ones where freedom is little more than a word, and a phony, tinny word at that.

These important people don't walk down the sidewalk in the bright sunshine. They ride from place to place in limousines with a crowd of burly men in dark suits shuffling them in and out of buildings. No limousines were parked on Gold Street. Only a red and white compact car across the street from Valliant Printing and the building with a sign that says "Available," and the United States senator from New Mexico, chairman of the Senate Budget Committee, gathering up briefcases and papers, walking down Gold Street with his back to the wind.

I thought of a poem Carl Sandburg wrote about a famous man he saw in a restaurant. This man had his picture on the front pages of newspapers; he bossed the work of thousands. But Sandburg said he saw him "eating soup, with a spoon."

Pete V. Domenici is an important person. Probably eats soup with a spoon, too. He's certainly in the newspaper a lot. One story had a headline that asked, "Domenici for Vice President?"

That got me to thinking about Pete V. Domenici becoming vice president. What are some of the things that happen when you get to be vice president or even president? Well, I don't know. I can only guess. I can only remember the story I was told by an old Washington correspondent about Harry Truman and Dean Acheson.

One Saturday afternoon Truman met with Acheson on some matter of diplomacy. When the meeting was over, Truman asked Acheson to stay, just to shoot the breeze. Truman wanted to go outside for a walk, but said he didn't dare because reporters would start shouting questions at him. So he asked Acheson to chew the fat for a while, because Bess and Margaret were in Independence, and at the moment the President of the United States was lonely and in need of another human being to jaw with.

I would guess that there are no red and white compact cars when you get to be president or vice president. Only limousines, and crowds of burly men in dark suits, hustling you out of a building, hustling you through a crowd, hustling you to a waiting car with window shades drawn, hustling you to the next hustling.

When you get to be president or vice president, your status as a person is permanently suspended. Even if you want to walk in the rain or the sunshine or down Gold Street with your back to the wind, you aren't allowed.

It doesn't seem to make a difference who's president or vice president, your connection to normality is severed. Although if you were out of touch to begin with, it probably eases the transition. And maybe it's not that way at all. Maybe Harry Truman was the exception. A lot of money is spent and lot of energy expended to be the person whose connection to normality is severed. Some people hunger for it.

Maybe this is nothing more than a set of naive questions caused by seeing Pete V. Domenici, United States senator and chairman of the Senate Budget Committee, who's been in *Time* and *Newsweek* and on coast-to-coast television, walking down Gold Street in the bright sunshine.

The wind mussed his hair.

25

If Nominated . . .

Thank you, but no, I will not run. I will not seek office and I will not accept the nomination. It's nice of you to ask.

Tough decisions and power over people's lives don't bother me. With a little practice and the right public relations man anybody can handle those problems.

It's the news coverage I can't cope with. It's the microscopic examination of every minute of my day that I can't handle.

I have been reading the papers and magazines. I have been watching TV and listening to the radio. An election is coming and I've been a good citizen, keeping informed so I can vote intelligently.

CANDIDATE ONE went shopping. I know what she wore, what she bought, where she bought it, how many bags it filled, who carried the bags, and how much (itemized list if I watch PBS) everything cost.

CANDIDATE TWO went fishing. On the first day he caught nothing, a fact duly reported and bounced off every available satellite. On the second day, he caught a few fish, another "news" story bounced off every available satellite so the villagers in Katsandkoo, India, would know the candidate caught a walleye.

I've been thinking about how my life would change should I accept the nomination. In just the past week or so, everyone would know a few things about me.

SUNDAY   The candidate went fishing in the San Juan quality waters, where he caught the largest trout he has ever caught in his woebegone fishing life. Because the trout measured sixteen inches long and not eighteen inches (the minimum keeper size), and because the candidate looked over his shoulder and saw the milling press contingent recording the event, the candidate released the fish—the largest, fattest, most wonderful fish he had ever caught in his life. The candidate, maintaining his support for honesty in government, fishing, poker games and most other places, cried like a baby after releasing the trout.

While on the same fishing trip, the candidate, after discovering his ancient waders leaked like the majority of the current White House staff, donned his hiking shorts and continued to fish. He bravely waded into the cold waters, incurring severe circulatory problems in the lower parts of his legs and sunburn on the upper parts of his legs. (The sunburn, unlike the trout, was a keeper.) The candidate then held a brief, streamside press conference in which he intensified his call for an investigation into the sun-block lotion industry.

MONDAY   The candidate made an appointment to have his teeth cleaned. He called for more teeth cleaning in America, saying it would lead to better health and a slimmer nation. He says teeth cleaning is the ultimate diet aid because his dental hygienist continually refers to "food debris" in the candidate's mouth. For weeks after having his teeth cleaned, the candidate cannot eat, because every time he tries to eat, all he can see before him is a plate full of potential food debris.

TUESDAY   The candidate spent a relaxing afternoon in his garden. After viewing the results of his summerlong effort, he called his insurance agent to see if the policy's act-of-God disaster coverage included that area of his back yard. The candidate's press secretary has issued a statement saying that after viewing his garden, the candidate is reassessing his opposition to agricultural price supports.

WEDNESDAY   The candidate went grocery shopping today. At the checkout stand, it occurred to him that he was about to pay $72.39 for a cart full of food debris. Cursing his dental hygienist, the candidate returned the food debris to the shelves.

FRIDAY   The candidate did nothing today. Political columnists and editorial writers are still assessing the impact. While waiting out the media reaction, the candidate fed his cat, making it clear that the cat's dinner would be the only photo opportunity of the day.

SATURDAY   The candidate, his eyes bloodshot, his voice raspy and weak, wearily addressed reporters early this morning as he stepped from the shower. The grim-faced nominee refused to answer questions, limiting the appearance to a single, terse statement: "The polls say I'm winning? Oh, God. . . ."

26

Old Snow

It's gone. The snow is gone. This is good. I want the snow to stay away. I'm much better about snow when it isn't around. I'm snow's master when it doesn't show up. I have my merit badges from many frigid Midwest winters. I'll tell everyone about them at the drop of a flake.

Snow? I say. You call this snow? Two inches? This is nothing, I tell the natives, especially the natives from southern New Mexico. You lilies, I say. Look at the way you people drive on this little bit of snow. I say this every time it snows, every time it looks like it might snow.

Then I hope nobody rides with me on the snowy streets, because this snow is not quite the same as the snow in my memory.

Oh, you should have seen the winter of '66, I'll tell them. Twenty-eight inches of snow in 24 hours. Did it stop us? No way. Slowed us down for a day or two, but we kept going.

You call this cold? This isn't cold. Sixteen below is cold. But it never bothered us. When we had to thaw out the garage door lock with a lighter, we didn't gripe. Our newspapers wrote editorials about how tough we were and how soft the rest of the country was. We loved it. Frigid, windy, snowy, sub-zero and we loved it.

I creep along the streets of Albuquerque, thinking about how much better the old snow was than this snow. This new snow isn't the same. My car slithers sideways and bumps the curb in this snow. Wheels spin, brakes lock, the car goes into an uncontrollable skid, and I'm glad nobody is with me to see it.

What is it about this snow that's different from the snow of my memory?

I know I'm not alone on this question. I have heard others laugh the same way I laugh. They say the same things about driving on snow that I say, but now that I think about it, I've never ridden with them when they're driving on snow.

When I sit in my house at night, pondering the eerie reflection of the corner street light on the snowscape, I am comfortable. I'm master of this snow. This is the same snow that falls in my mind. No problem with this snow. This snow is nothing, I say. I stand in my living room, pull the drapes open and launch into one more moving soliloquy about the snow.

In the morning, as I am dressing, I look out on the snow once again, shaking my head and smiling at the amusing snowphobia of the natives.

Boy, if they think this is snow . . . I'm thinking as the car engine warms up and I brush the snow from the windshield.

Moments later my car is sliding. I'm braking. The car should be stopping, but it's not, it's sliding. It never slid in those blizzards. I remember those blizzards as if they happened yesterday. I tell people about them all the time. My car never slid in those blizzards the way it's sliding now.

Blizzards were *de rigueur,* I say. Blizzards were standard operating procedure. We toughed it out. We kept on going. Nothing stopped us. A little snow never bothered us, I tell the natives, always reminding them that they missed something important in life because they never lived through months of snow and ice.

A friend said, "I was watching the news the other night. One of those midwesterners said, 'Sure it's eight below. Sure there's two feet of snow. Leave? Nah, I'll never leave. I love it. It doesn't bother me.' "

Of course, I say. That's absoslutely right. We're proud of that. A little snow doesn't bother us. We know how to handle it, how to drive on it. I did it for years.

But there was something different about that snow and the

snow under my tires this morning. It must be the altitude. That has to be it. The altitude makes this snow more slippery. The snow in my memory wasn't nearly as slippery as this snow because that old snow was closer to sea level. Sea-level snow was a snap.

Look at these people. Chugging along, afraid of a little snow and ice. Why, if they ever saw real snow, deep snow, and real ice, a genuine ice storm, if they ever saw the snow and ice I remember, the snow and ice that never bothered us . . .

I'm glad the snow is gone. This new snow wasn't at all like the old snow I remember. I'll tell you about it at the drop of a flake. We were the masters of that snow. Didn't bother us.

27

Tom's Truck

Tom's truck has 187,000 miles on it. This is not a testimonial to his mechanical ability—which extends just beyond turning the ignition key—but it does speak well of his choice of mechanics, such as the three he found in the parking lot of a liquor store.

It was 9:30 A.M. and already hot. Tom and his wife, Sarah, found a sitter for their daughter, and the day was meticulously planned for half a dozen errands, the first being at the liquor store. Tom made his purchase, returned to the truck, turned the ignition key, and nothing happened. After several more tries, he went back inside the liquor store. The clerk offered to jump-start the truck. It didn't work.

Then the beat-up yellow car with its three occupants appeared in the parking lot.

"It was pretty obvious they had come to stock up for breakfast," Tom says. "They were pretty 'happy.'"

The driver got out, surveyed the situation, and offered to help. "Gimme a six-pack and I'll fix it," he said.

"I told him we were calling a mechanic," Tom says. "He followed us into the store, got a fifth of vodka, and came up to the counter just as the clerk said he couldn't contact his mechanic friend. So this guy, who was the most solemn of the three, made another offer. 'If I don't fix it, you don't have to buy me anything,' he said. I figured, what the hell? Why not?"

Solemn went outside and said to his friends, "Get the tools out from under the seat."

From under the front seat of the beat-up yellow car came wrenches, screwdrivers, and wires. Solemn located the proper wrench to loosen the battery cables. He cleaned the battery posts. He hooked up the jumper cables. The key was turned. Nothing happened.

"Let's check the solenoid," Solemn said.

Solemn looked at the solenoid. "It's the solenoid," he declared, and his colleagues, each leaning on a fender, nodded—solemnly.

"I felt like they just told me my left ventricle was diseased," Tom says.

"Check under the seat," Solemn said. They went to the beat-up yellow car and checked under the seat. They returned with a solenoid. Brand new. It matched. "Perfect," Solemn declared.

"I didn't ask why they had a solenoid," Tom says. "I figured they'd have everything under that seat but a rear axle."

But they didn't have the right wrench. They checked under the seat. They checked in the trunk. No wrench. Lots of empty vodka bottles. No wrench.

Gloom descended on the hot parking lot—until the well-dressed, professional-looking woman drove in. Solemn and his colleagues made a rush for her. "You got a ³/₈ wrench?" they hollered.

She tried to avoid them, not at all sure of their intentions, but then stopped near the liquor store entrance, apparently deciding assault was not in the picture. "No," she said, returning to her car and retrieving a huge pair of pliers. "But I do have these."

A minor celebration ensued. Then back to work.

After some difficulty, the solenoid was replaced. Now they were ready. Solemn announced he would give the battery-cable nut one more turn for luck. He gave the nut the turn, and broke the battery cable. It was hot. The gloom was thick.

Solemn announced the need for a new terminal. Tom gave him five bucks. Solemn left a colleague as collateral.

Solemn's drinking buddy told Tom his life story, allowed as how drinking in parks is preferable to bars, said raw eggs are good for hangovers, and that his friends were good friends, great friends, the best of friends. Solemn's great and good friend increased the frequency of these evaluations as time dragged on and his great and good friends hadn't returned. He told Tom they'd be back any minute. He was sure of it.

Thirty minutes later they are back. The new battery terminal is installed. The truck starts. Another celebration ensues. Tom tells them to keep the change on the terminal, pays for the solenoid, and throws in a case of beer.

Solemn and his colleagues are happy and so is Tom—until the next errand, which is picking up his almost-new car, which was taken to the dealership because of a funny noise. He pays the dealership more than he paid Solemn. Halfway home the noise returns.

The truck still runs. The car still has the noise. And Tom cruises Albuquerque, his eyes peeled for a beat-up yellow car with empty vodka bottles, new solenoids, and everything but a rear axle under the front seat.

28

The Midway

I wasn't going to the State Fair this year. But I went. I figured it would just be more of the same. It was. I figured I'd just have to make that screwy time adjustment, the one where you enter a world whose population has a median age of 14. Of course, it happened. It happened as soon as I started weaving through the crust of midway humanity that swaggered and squealed its way up and down walkways that are never wide enough.

Everybody was there.

The overdeveloped 14-year-old girls in tube tops and shorts were there, flaunting their overdevelopment as if they really knew what to do with it. And wherever there are overdeveloped girls, there are underdeveloped boys, standing in line for the bus at the shopping center, smoking, cursing, making it clear they didn't give a damn what that dippy bus driver said. If the bus was full, they'd stand in the aisle, because they weren't about to wait another ninety seconds for the next bus to leave. Punctuating their big talk with a litany of obscenities, they flaunted their ignorance of what's cool and with it.

The portly, middle-aged woman in the tank top was there. She came down the midway with a husband and a kid flanking her. With each step, her body's rolls and folds gently maneuvered for breathing room within the constraints of the tank top—proving to all who cared to notice that you can't flaunt the unflauntable.

The guy with the suitcase stereo was there. He carried a monstrous radio-stereo-tape-deck model, the biggest one I ever saw. A Samonsite stereo. (I wondered if it was the same kind that the gorilla bounced around in his cage on the television commercial.) He lugged this thing along, volume cranked up, doing everything he could to compete with the loudspeakers blaring rock and roll from the midway rides. My God, I thought, he's taking them on. He cranks up the suitcase to ten and almost smokes 'em, but it's really a draw, which isn't bad considering the midway's amplification advantage. He hangs around for a minute or two and then moves on to a quieter part of the fairgrounds, a part where everybody can listen to his suitcase.

The televisions are turned on at the KOB-TV pavilion. This is where they do the nightly news live from the fairgrounds, where Dick Knipfing solemnly intones the day's disasters, Henry Tafoya unsolemnly reads the baseball scores and Bill Eisenhood points at a weather map. While they're doing this, there's a mob standing behind them, on camera, live, jumping up and down and waving and laughing. The mob, in theatrical parlance, is upstage of the stars, and the mob is having a hell of a good time upstaging them.

The news ends and a movie is shown on all three screens. Parents with children stand and watch the movie. They probably didn't want to come to the fair in the first place. "We'll go to the rides," a parent says. "Wait until the next commercial."

At the midway a carny spots a mark. "Fifty cents for three throws. Put one through and you win a prize." The mark plops down half a buck, grabs three taped-up rolls of toilet paper and pitches a roll through one of the three toilet seats hanging in the rear of the concession.

"A winner!"

Behind the winner, the mob slowly moves up and down the midway. Some of them, the young men with black T-shirts, tattoos, greasy jeans, scuffed boots and unfriendly eyes make me wonder where they are in this city the rest of the year, and how I might avoid them.

There is a teenage couple at the bus loading area; they wait arm in arm, then arms in arms, then kissing lightly, then kissing passionately, and then the whole world is phased out in a hugging, touching, kissing, fondling fog. The other fifty people in the line waiting for the bus back to the shopping center glance briefly and look away. The line moves. The couple moves with it, arm in arm, still kissing. They board the bus and hold hands. They kiss all the way to the shopping center. From the look of them they may not stop kissing by Monday and go to school.

I don't know why I go to the State Fair. I wasn't going to. I knew it would be more of the same. It was. I still went. I'll probably go again next year.

29
February

February is a miserable excuse for a month. Trying to salvage something useful out of February is like sending an eighth grade civics class on a field trip to Santa Fe to write essays on how legislative compromise is the grease that turns government's wheels.

Even February's name is wrong. What other month has a useless letter? No other month. Only February, with the first, extraneous, irrelevant, cosmetic *r*, sitting there in the middle of the word like a zit at the end of your nose.

Do you know anybody who pronounces February with that *r*? Of course you don't. We all say Feb-u-ary. Say it with that extra *r* and someone will slip you the business card of his brother-in-law, the speech therapist.

That useless *r* also makes February the most misspelled month, and it deserves it. Its misspelling is a sort of identification card for the year's most wasted twenty-eight days, or twenty-nine, depending on the year—which is another problem with February. It can't seem to settle on the number of days it wants. The only explanation for this must be that whoever invented the month realized the foolishness of it and quit before getting to the standard thirty or thirty-one.

Not much happens in the way of holidays in February.

Oh, there's Valentine's Day, but that's not in the big leagues with Christmas, New Year's, Thanksgiving, Independence Day, Memorial Day and Labor Day. We send cards on Valentine's Day, but do we get the day off? Of course not.

Two of our most revered presidents were born in February, but February is so unremarkable that we don't bother with their birthdays anymore. It's been so long since we celebrated their birthdays, nobody remembers the dates. We just know Lincoln and Washington were born on the same day—a Monday between Feb. 12 and Feb. 22. We call this day Presidents' Day and some of us celebrate by not going to work, which is something all of us might consider as a solution to the whole month.

February is head cold month. People who made it through winter's most bitter days without so much as a sniffle spend all of February trying to breathe and wondering if they will ever again eat solid food.

November leaves us with the taste of turkey and pumpkin pie; December's posole lingers into January, when we cozy up in front of a fire and sip hot buttered rum.

February's dominant taste is vapor-action cough drops.

February is a faker. January might be cold, but we expect it to be cold. When it's cold in January, it's no big deal. March will be windy. We know it for sure, so when the winds come, we are not surprised or out of sorts because March is windy.

But February fakes. Every February, usually in the middle of this alleged month, the temperature warms and the air has the feeling of spring. Foolish people, tired of winter, rush outside to marvel at an early-blooming flower. Suffering from winter's cabin fever, we fall for February's practical joke every time. We clean, dig, plant, sit out on the patio and think . . . *At last, another winter is gone.* Within thirty-six hours of thinking this, the freeze returns, the fruit trees are shot, the flowers wilt and February is laughing its extra *r* off.

This is because February has faked us out again. It isn't spring. It's not even close to spring. . . except in Arizona and Florida . . . where baseball players are beginning to loosen up during the first days of spring training . . . which begins every February . . . and is the first sign of a new baseball season . . . which could make February just about the most marvelous month of the whole year.

90

30

The *Times*

I have been quoted in the *New York Times*. Yes, the one in New York, the one at 229 West 43rd St. All of the News That's Fit to Print. Without Fear or Favor. The Big Leagues. The Summit. Awed reverence and all that. The only problem is that the day my name was in the *New York Times* it must have been foggy on Olympus.

A few weeks ago the American Civil Liberties Union in Albuquerque said it wanted the cross removed from the Bernalillo County seal. What with book burnings, censorship, television news and orange barrels, I thought the ACLU probably had better things to do. So I wrote a column about the Bernalillo County seal. That's when the *New York Times* came along.

The *Times* Albuquerque correspondent wrote what she thought was a tongue-in-cheek story and called it in. I talked to her about it after the story appeared in the *Times*. She was sure she made it clear that I wasn't serious, which goes to show what the *Times* correspondent knows about the *Times*. She quoted some things I said in the column. Now she and I know something about the *New York Times* that we didn't know before: When writing a tongue-in-cheek story for the *Times*, you have to punch your tongue clean through your face before the *Times* gets the joke.

I know the *Times* isn't much to laugh at. Once you get past Russell Baker, things get serious, and sometimes even solemn.

I know a man who worked in Washington for many years and his work was widely respected. He said people often had the mistaken impression that he worked for the *Times*, when in fact he worked for the Associated Press. His wife joked that it happened because he was always serious. This impression of seriousness was so strong that the *Times* once offered him a job, but he turned it down, because upon reflection, he decided that even he wasn't serious enough for the *Times*.

Anyway, there was some rewriting done to the Albuquerque correspondent's story and this is what it said the day my name showed up in the *New York Times,* the *New York* Sunday *Times,* by the way, the one that everyone has time to read, the one that goes all over the country, all over the world, to presidents and prime ministers and diplomats and even the Russians, for God's sake.

"The ACLU move has the support of Jim Arnholz of the Albuquerque Journal, a morning newspaper in this county seat of 350,000. He said he once pulled up beside a county vehicle at a stoplight and felt an uncontrollable urge to go to confession."

Well, there it is. And it's true. I said it. I wrote that the influence of the Bernalillo County seal, with its cross staring at me from the side of a dump truck, was so strong it gave me an uncontrollable urge to go to confession. I cannot deny I wrote that.

But I was kidding, see? That line about wanting to go to confession because of the cross on the county seal and all that? I didn't mean it. I thought the ACLU could find more important things to do, so I wrote . . . Well, I wrote what I wrote, and now I want to holler up to the top of the mountain, up there to Olympus where they toil with all the news that's fit to print without fear or favor. I want to holler, "IT WAS ONLY A JOKE, GUYS!"

This is terrible. I don't like complaining about the *Times.* Other people say they have been had by the *Times.* Richard Nixon, Spiro Agnew, guys like that. Who wants to be in that crowd?

A few days after that story ran, I met a friend coming out of a movie theater. "Hey," he said, "I was in Philadelphia over the weekend and I was reading the *Times.* I saw your name in that story on the cross and the county seal. Did you really mean . . ."

No, I said, I didn't mean it. I was kidding. I wasn't serious. I can't figure out how they thought I was serious.

It was nice seeing my name in the *New York Times*. That was fun. They spelled it right, too . . . but I sure do wish someone had looked at that story . . . again.

I didn't mean it, guys. Honest, I didn't. I was kidding.

31

Blessed Are
the Unhandy

Being unhandy is . . . well, unhandy. The unhandy's alternatives are limited to (a) don't fix it, or (b) prostrate yourself at the feet of the handy and suffer the humiliation of not even knowing why something is broken, let alone offering an opinion on how to fix it.

For the unhandy, the most chilling words in the English language are "do it yourself." This ugly unhandy reality is without exception—except for the exception of paint. Paint is the salvation of the unhandy. Paint is the secret island to which the unhandy may retreat.

No hula girls sway on this island. There are no palm trees or sandy beaches. Only rollers, brushes, paint chippers, a can of spackling and (if you're smart about what kind of paint you buy) a little water for cleaning-up purposes.

Except for paint, the world of the handy offers nothing for the unhandy. I know, just as millions of other unhandy people know, that mechanics, carpenters, plumbers and electricians operate in a closed world. It is a world populated primarily by men who carry numerous pens and mechanical pencils in shirt-pocket pen caddies. Small scissors in leather carrying cases are held fast to their belts. Look for the men wearing not clip-on ties, but clip-on tape measures and you are among the handy.

The handy's language is a foreign one, but the unhandy have learned the telltale clue to identifying the handy: The handy are unable to express themselves mathematically unless a fraction is used. Listen to someone say 1, 35, 57, or 628 and it's a sure bet you are listening to someone who is unhandy, but if the numbers are $^3/_8$ or $^5/_{16}$, you've got yourself a handyman.

Spot somebody with a sawdust-covered baseball cap and a tire gauge stuck in the pen caddy with all the pens and pencils, and he is handy, and to be avoided. He's the kind of guy who points to the 1,200-square-foot addition on his house and says, "Oh, that? Just something I threw together last summer."

We, the unhandy, don't fix things. We don't fix cars, for instance. I tried once. I changed the spark plugs. Then I called a friend to help me start the car.

"Did you put them in the proper firing order?" he said.

Tell me what a firing order is, I answered, and I'll tell you if I did it.

That was the last time I tried to fix a car, but I still paint. Give me a wall, a roller, a can of paint and I become the homeowner's Michelangelo.

Anything beyond paint intimidates me. Oh, I repaired a bathroom wall once. Replastered and tiled the thing. It went all right if you don't count the gentle curve in the wall that mysteriously appeared right after I laid the last tile. Once in a while a visitor will notice the softly curving shower wall and ask about it. Adobe shower, I say to the visitor. Quaintly New Mexican, don't you think?

Painting, though, is a dream. Roll it on, mess it up, roll over it and nobody knows the difference. The house reeks of paint, the sweet, acrid, nostril-assaulting smell of success. When I paint, I always remember to open several windows, but I don't open them for proper ventilation; I open them so the whole neighborhood knows I'm doing something handy.

I can paint for days, and I have just finished painting for days. Seven of them, seven straight days in which I almost painted the whole house. Now it looks like new. Smells like new, too.

The dining room shines, and except for the closet doorknob that wouldn't turn after I put it back on, the dining room is done. The den looks as if it were built yesterday, and if the wall anchors holding the bookshelves hadn't ripped out of the plaster under the weight of the books, sending everything crashing down, the den would be done. The kitchen looks great, and as soon as I put on the new wallpaper, it will be even better. I wasn't going to change the wallpaper, but when I was through painting and I pulled off the masking tape, the wallpaper came with it.

These are but small matters, though. I never claimed to be handy. But I can paint.

32

Bike Trail

Not enough miles have passed under the wheels of my new bicycle for me to claim any wondrous benefits from exercise. To be truthful, I prefer cruising downhill to chugging up. Still, there has been a payoff already, first time I took the bike out, as a matter of fact.

I set out on a bike path that follows a concrete arroyo through the city. Almost immediately it seemed not so different from driving down a country road. What came to mind was U.S. 54, through the Tularosa Basin. Whenever I go south, I take U.S. 54, not I-25. For one thing, it's prettier, and for another, friendlier. Drive that old two-lane highway and a most uncitified occurrence is commonplace. People wave; people in cars and trucks wave. They don't wave on I-25, just as they don't wave on Gibson or Montgomery or Isleta or Rio Grande. Strange behavior in the city, made even stranger when the bike path intersects a major roadway. The faces in automobiles look different from the faces on the bike path. They seem to confirm a description I saw years ago in a book. The author said everything a car driver sees is nothing but more television. The driver isn't part of the scene; he's removed from it.

The bike rider is *in* the scene, which is far better, but creates a problem. There is a terrible danger for the bike rider. He has a tendency to feel just a little superior. You know . . . clean living, in touch with the world, not polluting . . . all that. This superiority is tempered only when the bike rider remembers that if he isn't careful when crossing the intersection, his motorized inferiors will hardly notice when they add him to the bug collections on their windshields.

This was still part of the payoff, though. If nothing else, it showed there was life in the slow lane. The big payoff came in a dirt field behind a school. That's where the kids were playing what can only be called "soccball" or "baseoccer." I've often wondered if kids still make up games, unsupervised by adults, unorganized, no uniforms, no coaches, no cheering parents, no cursing parents, no browbeating parents, no parents who have failed to notice that God made only one Vince Lombardi and the one He made died many years ago.

At any rate, I didn't know if kids still hung around after school playing made-up, jerry-built games. Now I know. They do.

Fields behind schools are considerably more attractive when the school day is over, especially in fall, on a cloudy day. There is a distinctly different feeling about that field on an overcast fall day, a feeling even better than in summer, when there's no school day to plow through.

The light is gray; the school silent, save for the seven boys and two girls on the dirt field. The game is a hybrid of soccer and baseball. There are fielders, a pitcher, bases, a batter who's really a kicker, and an orange, black-spotted soccer ball that the pitcher rolls to home plate. The hitter kicks the ball and the game is on. There's a lot of yelling, a lot of running, and a little arguing, but it isn't the same kind of arguing that goes on with adult supervision. The arguing is unsupervised, uninterrupted by older, more expert arguers. The rhubarbs are brief and marked by voices that reach higher and higher and higher, until they crack, a sure yardstick for measuring the debaters' years and convictions.

There is the liberal male contingent, saying the little girl was so safe that the blindest of idiots should have seen it; there's the conservative male contingent, saying she obviously was out and besides, she's a girl and doesn't know what she's doing anyway; and there's the female contingent, quickly tiring of the whole thing, and walking away to leave the cracking male voices to crack by themselves.

Whatever happens, the game goes on. I don't know what

the score was or if it mattered enough to keep. It was a good game, the kind of game that goes on as the day grows grayer and grayer, finally turning to darkness so complete nobody can see the ball he's supposed to hit, or in this case, kick. Only then do the players straggle from the field and head for home.

As I left, they were still playing that hybrid game in the dust of a grassless field behind the school. I cruised away on my new bicycle, downhill, all the way home. It was good exercise.

33

Guitar Player

Almost every day at lunchtime, the guitar-strumming singer sits at the apex of a grassy, concrete-walled triangle in the Fourth Street pedestrian mall. The lunchtime crowd squeezes itself toward the cool shade of the mall's east side. As the lunch hour rolls on, the tanned singer finds himself in the noonday sun.

He pinches off the glowing ash of a cigarette and drops the filter into an empty Camel pack, a habit of his Air Force training, when he learned all cigarettes are "field stripped"—paper shredded and dropped into a shirt pocket, tobacco left to blow in the wind.

He launches into a slow ballad. The guitar and his voice, gently amplified through two microphones and a small speaker, seem to fit in with the urban sounds of the chugging cars, trucks and buses, the conversation of downtown workers, the shuffling of feet moving up and down the mall.

A young man in a T-shirt and cut-off blue jeans approaches. He smiles, digs into a pocket of his cut-offs and pulls out some change. He drops it into the blue canvas guitar case.

"Thanks," Rick Best says, momentarily interrupting a song. A short man with an ample middle walks by. He's carrying a burlap bag. He stops at one of the squat trash receptacles in the mall, fishes out aluminum cans, drops them in his burlap bag and moves on, not giving so much as a glance at the singer.

Rick Best is singing a Johnny Cash railroad song when a man in his mid-30s, wearing a three-piece suit, and having tremendous potential as a Yuppie poster child, walks by. He looks askance at the singer, trying to see without being seen

The singer is dressed in blue jeans, a long-sleeved shirt with the sleeves rolled up and scuffed black boots, old friends that have tapped to many a song. The Yuppie looks as if he's trying to make a connection, trying to find something in his memory that will explain this lean, long-haired man singing on the Fourth Street pedestrian mall. The connection, whether the Yuppie knows it or not, is there.

Rick Best's singing career is considerably shorter (eighteen months) than was his computer career (twenty years). His singing career, supplemented by a job in a downtown cabinet shop, provides far less income than did his computer job. The difference between a computer career and singing career is immense. He's glad he sought out the difference.

"I started singing here about a month and half ago," Rick says. "When I started, people didn't quite know what to do with me. For three days I would see people looking at me. I'd look back, smile, and they'd look away, like they'd been caught spying. It's nice now, though. I've got an awful lot of nameless friends."

He began his singing career in New York, when a friend in the entertainment business invited him to give it a try. He stayed in New York only three months and then returned to Albuquerque.

"It was a lot easier when I came back," he says. "I didn't have to make the decision about getting out of computers. I was already out. All I had to do was decide to stay out."

Three men walk by. One smiles and calls out, "How can you smoke and play and sing at the same time?" Rick laughs and points to the neck of the six-string guitar. The cigarette, rigidly perpendicular to the instrument, is held fast under the guitar strings.

Making the move from the safety of a twenty-year computer career to the unpredictable fortunes of songwriting and singing wasn't easy. It falls into that general category of "Things I Wish I'd Done." Rick Best removed the "I wish."

"One day this distinguished gentleman came by," he says. "He was wearing a three-piece suit and carrying a briefcase.

He walked up to me and stuffed a dollar bill in my shirt. I wondered, *What kind of secret dreams does he have? What did he let pass him by?* I appreciate that; I did it for twenty years in computers. Now I sing in this little park. Now I have that enjoyment."

34

Oh, Tannenbaum!
Oh, Tannenbaum!

Such Christmas trees! The nursery had a warehouse full of perfect, I mean to say, *perfect* Christmas trees. The first one I looked at cost $38.

I moved on: $32, $35, $47, $34. I moved on, and out, out of the nursery, back to the car, driving too slowly on a crowded boulevard, backing up mean, angry, unseasonal-like traffic behind me, looking for Christmas tree lots, thinking that maybe this would be the year principle gives way to common sense and I buy a phony, plastic, perfect, utterly-without-a-flaw tree.

I pulled into a lot. A guy with a baseball cap that had an "Oregon" patch on it watched as I walked along the tree aisles: $29, $31, $46.

I moved on. A little farther down San Mateo I saw another sign: "Christmas Trees! Mora, New Mexico." Oh, well, if my tree's price is to be inflated, it might as well be inflated by neighbors. No price tags adorn the trees. After a few minutes of wandering, I find my tree, full but flawed, but who's perfect? A guy in a down jumpsuit and a battered black cowboy hat approaches. I ask him how much.

"Three to five bucks a foot."

What's three and what's five?

"Depends on the tree."

How about this one?

He looks over the tree and gives me a price, then drops the price two bucks. I drop it another two bucks. He says OK. I give him the money and hoist the tree to my shoulder. As I leave the lot, the Mora tree seller sings out, "Merry

Christmas! I'll be here next year, too. Be sure to come back. Merry Christmas!"

I drive home, feeling good about the mass of needled greenery that fills my rear view mirror; I'm feeling Christmasy, filled with the spirit of the season and wondering why I didn't have the sense to go for another two bucks off the price. But the money is no big deal. This is Christmas. I'm feeling full of tradition.

At home, I make myself a traditional hot buttered rum and begin yet another Christmas tradition: tearing apart the garage trying to find the Christmas tree stand. The tree is placed in the stand and rises in all its Mora majesty. Out come the lights, and out go the lights. The first strand is plugged in and tested. Perfect. The second strand is plugged in and tested. Not perfect. In fact, nothing at all. Black. Dead as a doornail.

The cat, who's as much a traditionalist as I am, comes in to check out the tree.

"Get outa here, Walter. There's not even an ornament on to knock off yet."

The cat hovers under the tree, his nose mashed into a branch. "Get outa here!"

This command brings two immediate and inevitable results. The cat leaves and the dog wakes up, wandering over to see what's going on. He sniffs the base of the tree, sniffs again, turns in a semi-circle, sniffs again, begins to lift his—

"No!"

The dog leaves.

It's time for another traditional hot buttered rum, but that means getting out the mix, measuring it, heating the water, and stirring everything. Lucky for me another longstanding Christmas tradition in my family is rum and Diet Shasta Cola. It gets me back to the tree sooner.

Out come the ornaments—the best part. Christmas tree ornaments are like old friends you see once a year. Some go back a long way; some are relative newcomers; some are looked for, sought out before the others; some are vaguely familiar and raise questions about why they were bought in the first place.

By the time the ornaments are in place, it's late, the end of a long day and night. Time for one last traditional rum and Diet Shasta Cola. I lie back on the couch and admire yet another magnificent tree. I'm feeling just about as Christmasy as is humanly possible. I close my eyes and I can almost hear the faint tinkling of Christmas bells.

In fact, I *can* hear the tinkling of small glass bells as they are batted around the tree branches by that damn cat.

"Get outa here!"

35

From the bottom of the Christmas Tree

When hot air balloons are inflated, when those first gusts of air are forced into the envelopes, kneading them into the lumpy bulges that precede mature growth, it's as if the wildest dreams of a mad scientist—in this case, a botanist—have come true. It's as if this loony botanist and his loony idea of making the desert bloom were exiled to a New Mexico mesa and told, "Call us if it works."

In the gray time between early-morning darkness and early-morning sun, hundreds of small fan motors begin chugging, giving the mesa the sound of the main display hall at a lawn-mower convention. The balloons begin to stir, begin to get the idea that it's time to get up.

Then comes the first blast of a propane gas burner, then another, and another, and soon the mesa is filled with the sound of so many half-awake dragons clearing their throats.

A slow, 360-degree turn in the middle of this mesa-turned-atrium, filled with billowing nylon bulbs, has the look of time-lapse photography, recording in minutes the days-long blooming of a flower garden. By the time the sun clears the jagged, black outline of the Sandias, many of these wildly-colored desert flowers are rising to meet it.

Conversations are shouted. Bystanders yell in delight to one another; amateur photographers squint through view-finders while amateur assistant photographers point in the opposite direction, grab an elbow and holler, "Get that! Get that!"; crews and pilots bellow directions, good lucks and good-byes.

All the while, more dragons awaken, more throats are cleared in a blast of gas and flame.

Earlier, in the darkness, conversations were morning conversations—quiet, no matter the number of people involved.

At 5:30 A.M., science fiction movies come to mind, otherworldly places where the only sound is that of a portable generator here and there. The field's light comes from portable units that define spaces in limited gray and infinite black.

Even at this early hour, long lines of spectators disgorge from buses heard but not seen. Some stand in the glare of the portable lights, some fade into the grayness, while the ends of the lines can't be seen, going from light to gray to gone in the blackness.

By 6 A.M., a sizable crowd mills around the midway, and make no mistake about it, because that's exactly what it is—a midway. This is a carnival. But not a carnival in the sense that the State Fair is a carnival. No barkers bark, no rides swirl through flashing lights, no music blares.

This carnival is primarily a participatory carnival consisting of spectators, crews, pilots, vendors, officials and anybody else who shows up. This carnival is the woman who paints long whiskers on her face and wears a hat with big bunny ears. This carnival is crazy, furry hats and silk jackets—bright, red and yellow and blue and green and pink and silver silk jackets laden with buttons and pins. This carnival is the balloon fiesta official in his official black-and-white striped referee's shirt—and his black-and-white striped shorts, and his black-and-white striped knee socks.

Every conversation begins with the same two words. There are no exceptions. At the food stands, information booths, souvenir stands, officials' trailers, even at the entrances to parking areas where orange-vested traffic "cops" wave in car after car, the greeting never changes: "Good morning!"

By 7:30 A.M., the first balloon flight leaves the mesa. Ground-bound necks crane skyward and the view is that of the ornaments on the Christmas tree's bottom branch, peering up at all the other bulbs and baubles.

In a way, it *is* Christmas. With each inflation, a new gift opens up. With each lift-off, the eyes have a new toy. It's Christmas in October. And a carnival at that.

36
Pie in the Sky

Pie stands alone. Pie is judged on its own merits. Pie isn't decorated. Cake is decorated. Pie is filled. You don't tiptoe around pie the way you tiptoe around cake. Cake is dessert's flower garden; pie is dessert's meat and potatoes. Marie Antoinette didn't say, "Let 'em eat pie," because if she had, everybody would have thought it was a good idea.

This isn't to say cake is without merit. Walk through the Creative Arts Center at the State Fair and you'll see cakes, all kinds of gorgeous cakes, the peacocks of the kitchen.

There are E.T. cakes, Big Bird cakes, flowery cakes, blue cakes, green cakes, pink cakes, red cakes, orange cakes, rainbow cakes, magnificent, stunning cakes that look as if they came from the kitchens of Salvador Dali and Jackson Pollock. All of them lovingly, artfully prepared.

But cake isn't pie, and Thursday was pie day at the State Fair, Thursday was pie *contest* day. Tables full of pies were lined up in the Creative Arts Center. Not a flashy pie was in sight. There were no E.T. pies, no surrealistic, gaudy-yellow Big Bird pies rising three feet above the table top. These pies were strawberry, peach, cherry, pecan, mincemeat, apple, rhubarb, and—blueberry, the King of Pies, the kind of pie that might be found in the sky.

No flash, no glitter. Everything in accordance with the official rules as clearly laid out in the official State Fair Pie Contest Rule Book—"No cream pies or whipped cream toppings." That's the way it should be in a pie contest. We don't want any pansy pies. No white-capped, banana cream pretenders to the throne need apply. All you meringue makers stay home and save your egg whites for another day.

Seats filled quickly, and as the judges began to slice the first pies—cherry and apple—the situation becomes Standing Room Only.

Sixty-five pies would be cut and tasted before the day was done. Think of it. Sixty-five kitchens soaking up pie smells; sixty-five sets of eyes cautiously peering through the glass in the oven doors.

Sturdy pies rested in heavy glass and metal pans. Set one down on a kitchen table and it replies with a *thunk!* Solid. Dependable.

What covers cake? Frosting. Say it slowly. Frossss . . . ting. Sounds like something a ballet critic might say.

What covers pie? *Crust!* The Earth has a *crust!* Uncle Charlie is *crusty!* Pies have *crust* . . . tender, flaky, but always stable, *crust!*

The judges are tough. An apple winner is named, but no first place is awarded to cherry. Then comes blueberry. The judges begin and the tension could be cut with a pie knife. (Don't even think of doing it with a cake cutter. It would bend under the pressure.)

When the home economist judge stands to speak, the words don't carry nearly the weight as the sound of her voice. She is excited, almost breathless; something has happened here that might set the home economics world on its ear. She has found a superb, dazzling blueberry pie.

"First place . . . Marion Isidoro!"

It turns out the pie is Marion Isidoro's first blueberry pie. The Albuquerque woman's intent had been peach.

"I was going to bake a peach pie, but the store was out of peaches," she said. "I decided to give blueberry a try. I think the difference was that I used fresh blueberries. My mother had them in her refrigerator and said if I wanted them, I was welcome to them."

Her champion pie was a thick but delicate brute with a tender, flaky crust and berries that exploded in your mouth with each bite . . .

Beg pardon? How do I know? Well, I got to talking with

Marion . . . and with the officials . . . and the judges took only two slices . . . which left an awful lot of pie that might have gone to waste . . .

Never mind. All this is beside the point. Take my word for it. Marion Isidoro makes an All-World Blueberry Pie.

Besides, one more hurdle remained in the State Fair pie contest: Best of Show. Best of apple, rhubarb, pecan, strawberry, peach, mincemeat and blueberry. The judges huddled, comparing notes, conferring more, heads nodded and the announcement was made. And the winner is . . . Marion Isidoro's All-World Blueberry Pie!

In your heart you knew it was right.

37

Ah, Autumn!

Summer fades. It began Saturday, at 6:33 P.M. to be exact—the Autumn Equinox.

Ah, autumn! The sun rises due east, a direction marked by the alignment of the Great Pyramid of Giza in Egypt. The sun illuminates Mayan temples in Guatemala and medicine wheel patterns arranged in stone by Plains Indians in the United States and Canada, and shines down on specially aligned graves in Ireland.

The green leaves of summer turn a blazing orange, teaming up with the glorious orange street barriers specially aligned by the Druids of the Orange Barrel Sect, to finally and properly color coordinate what's left of this city's streets.

Then the leaves will fall, gently fall, and fall and fall and fall, which is the other name we call autumn. And after falling and falling, they will pile up and pile up and pile up, and soon it will be winter, and then who cares about piled-up leaves? All the neighbors will be inside their homes, too traumatized by their gas bills to say snooty things about the leaves piled up in your yard.

Ah, autumn! No more lazy, hazy days of summer. No more gin and tonics in the shade, no more pool parties, no more trips to the lake, no more putting on a swim suit and wondering what in the name of all that is good and holy happened to your body. It used to be so . . .

Ah, autumn! Summer's blazing days are gone. Now a crackling fire awaits you and your significant other (known as your "honey" prior to the Psychobabble Revolution). A hot buttered rum for you, an Irish coffee for him/her (common pronoun usage recommended by three out of four leading psychobabblists).

Ah, autumn! Sweater weather. No more summertime, soft-core porn shows at the grocery store. As the harvest moon rises, the produce department clientele changes from its sumertime R rating to the PG-13 of fall and then, at long last, winter's bundled-up boring, but fine for the family, G-rated shopping trips.

Ah, autumn! A season of bounty, the forerunner of winter's chilly days, cold nights, network news film of blizzards across the nation, and you, comfortable, snug and smug, sitting in your easy chair, glancing out the window at the clear blue New Mexico sky, chuckling a mildly mean-spirited chuckle as you glance back at the televised blizzard and say, "Anything else on TV, honey?"

Ah, autumn! Summer is out; school is in; blazing colors, short days, long, romantic nights, footballs flying, golden aspens, frost on the pumpkins, the World Series . . . the World Series . . . the World Series is played . . . and it ends . . . and the baseball season is . . . over.

Ah, well, spring is just around the corner.

38

Running Shoes and Other Carcinogens

Good morning. Nice day, I hope. Having a leisurely Sunday breakfast? Good, sounds terrific. Already been out for the early morning jog? You have? That many miles? You don't say? Well, I hate to do this . . . it's not the kind of thing I generally crow about . . . but science, which always comes through if you wait long enough, has come through again. Researchers have tracked down proof of a theory I proposed long ago. Jogging causes cancer. I hate to say I told you so, but . . .

To be honest, it isn't just jogging. It's any kind of vigorous exercise, with the exception of vigorous eating, which causes cholesterol build-up, which causes heart attacks. Exercise releases something called "free radicals," which run around inside your body, damaging genetic material, DNA, membranes, proteins and deactivating or disrupting the functions of cells.

Medical researchers tested rats and guinea pigs by having them run on tiny treadmills. (I wonder what a rat thinks when he hits the wall of pain.) The rats and guinea pigs suffered immediate cell and tissue damage if they were deficient in vitamin E or had ingested too little or too much vitamin C.

I've been telling people about the dangers of jogging for years, but nobody would listen. Nobody took me seriously when I said the soles of every pair of running shoes should carry a warning from the surgeon general: "Caution: Carcinogenic shoes. Jog at your own risk."

Dr. Lester Packer, professor of physiology and anatomy at

the University of California at Berkeley, said, "Exercise may be good for shaping up the cardiovascular system and trimming potentially deadly body fat, but we have evidence it may affect other pathologies, leading to cancer and other diseases."

This news is not nearly as distressing as you might think, though.

Look, what's the point of exercise? Keep the heart in shape, right? Keep the old cholesterol levels low, right? Cut down the chances of cardiovascular disease, right?

Friends, low cholesteraol is fine if you don't want to die of a heart attack, but if you're worried about suicide or homicide . . . Well, a Finnish researcher now says low cholesterol cuts down your chances of heart attack, but increases your chances of impulsive homicidal and suicidal behavior.

Isn't it fun? You can eat all the eggs and pizza you want and fall over dead, or you can exercise and get cancer and fall over dead, or, if you're lucky, and don't get cancer, you can exercise, lower your cholesterol level and commit suicide, or kill your boss or mailman or whoever gets in the way on the day your cholesterol level hits rock bottom.

This Finnish researcher, in a letter to the *Journal of the American Medical Association,* said participants in a U.S. heart disease study who had low cholesterol levels were suicidal, homicidal and had a higher than expected rate of accidental and violent deaths.

However, this was not the case in other studies. (*Other studies* are what make medical news so much fun. All you need is a little patience and other studies will bail you out.) Anyway, other studies showed that people with low cholesterol levels weren't homicidal or suicidal, but merely irresponsible and lacking in self-control, which presumably, led to overeating and frequent heart attacks.

OK, let's review: Exercise and die from cancer; exercise and commit suicide, homicide or at the very least become irresponsible and lacking self-control; don't exercise and pig out while waiting for your myocardial infarction.

Everybody straight on that? Good. Now have another cinnamon roll and go read the comics.

39

Have a Nice Day, R.C.

The kind of success that brings fame and wealth also brings the IRS, but the IRS wants only a piece of the action, not a piece of you, unless, of course, it doesn't get a piece of the action.

Success brings another group, too; this group thrives on success, but not theirs, yours. All you have to do is succeed and the next thing you know, here they come, scudding along like hyenas late for lunch.

In *Impact,* the weekly magazine of the *Albuquerque Journal,* there appeared a nature story about these hyenas. The story was called "The Selling of R.C. Gorman." I've been waiting to see that story, waiting to see what the art world would have to say about this Navajo artist who isn't . . . well, who isn't pleasing the art world.

I knew the story was coming and even before it was in the works I had heard comments about "raging commercialism" in regard to Gorman and his art. A lot of people in the art world (which has nothing to do with the rest of the world) have gotten their noses out of joint about R.C. Gorman. What it comes down to is that R.C. is making a lot of money and having the time of his life. This unseemly artist behavior is driving the art world nuts. The art world can't stand it and I don't think they'd be happy even if Gorman donated his Mercedes to Hertz.

One comment I have heard about the famed Navajo painter was, "He's not showing any growth."

Like hell he isn't.

He's got a three-million-dollar house, two galleries, and a multi-million-dollar empire. Where I grew up that would be

considered reasonable growth, because where I grew up growth
often was demonstrated in the neighborhood by having two
six-packs instead of one on the front porch for those hot
summer nights.

Anyway, in this magazine story, a gallery owner offered
his views on the sins of R.C. Gorman. This guy runs a gallery
in—steady yourself—New York, the seat of all wisdom east
of the Hudson River. (If you care to check any decent eighth
grade geography book, you'll find that the world ends west
of it.)

He had some interesting things to say, one of my favorites
being that the majority of people who buy Gorman's lithographs are not real collectors; they're just average people.
Only the people who buy his originals know fine art.

I took this personally, because all along I thought I was
moving up in self-taught art appreciation and now it turns
out I'm not even average. Average people buy the lithographs,
but I don't, because I can't afford them, and I don't buy
originals, because I can't afford them, either. I do own two
Gorman posters, which must place me somewhere between
below average and beyond hope. As long as I have admitted
that I'm below average, I might as well go ahead and confess
why I bought the posters. I like them.

Nobody told me to buy them. Nobody told me what to
look for and why I should or shouldn't buy them. I bought
them for no other reason than I liked them. This was not a
complicated process. I looked at them and I said, "I like that."
I wouldn't know a Titian from a Matisse if somebody hit me
over the head with the frame; an art expert friend of mine
once said my idea of art was the cover of this week's *Sports
Illustrated*. But I looked at those Gorman posters, looked at
the price, decided I liked both, and wrote the check. That
may not hold a lot of water in the art world, but they look
nice in the living room, thank you.

Now, because I am always on the lookout for insights into
New Mexico Indians, and because New York art gallery own-

ers are known the world over as experts on New Mexico Indians, I want to take another look at a statement this New York Indian expert made.

He said Gorman went for the money, and that going for the money was "probably very Indian of him."

And all this time I thought it was the paleface art gallery owners who went for the money. The statement does, however, raise an interesting, if not important, question: What's wrong with Indians going for the money? Presumably, Fritz Scholder, another successful Indian artist, is less Indian than Gorman because Scholder didn't go for the money, although the last time I heard anything about him he seemed to be doing OK.

Maybe I should accept the New York gallery owner's statement at face value and let it go at that. After all, who am I to question pronouncements on New Mexico Indians made by an art gallery owner in New York?

Still, I never understood why poets, novelists, artists or anybody with an ounce of creativity has to be dead before he, or at least whoever's in the will, can reap any benefit from his talent. Why does the art world, or the book world, or any world populated by people who never wrote a book or painted a painting, get so bent out of shape when somebody makes money?

You want commercialization? Give me a call. I've got mounds of unpublished material sitting in a desk drawer at home. If anyone out there wants to commercialize it, by all means go right ahead and commercialize. We'll commercialize ourselves right into a Swiss chalet. We'll print novels and plays on cocktail napkins. I don't care.

Success is odd; people are all for it, until it happens to somebody else. In that terrible event, some way must be found to take the successful down a notch or two. Why else would the New York art gallery owner say Gorman doesn't do many originals because he's "lazy." I don't know if R.C. Gorman is lazy or not, but if I were R.C., I'd crank out another three hundred lithographs, sign them eight times, charge six times the going rate and build a $2 million gazebo in the backyard of that $3 million dollar house. He can keep his herd of sheep in it—for tax purposes, of course.

40

Collectibles

If you have time tonight, inventory a closet you haven't set foot in since 1971 or so. Poke around the garage and see what materializes. Make a list of everything you don't need, will never use again and haven't even thought of since you last moved (which is usually when these items appear and always lead to the question: Why am I keeping this?). When you figure out why you're keeping it (them?), let me know. Then maybe I'll know what to do with this expired passport, outdated Eurailpass, map of Europe, brochure on "15 Top Spots in Switzerland" and 550 lire. All of it was handy in 1977, but it's not 1977 anymore, and hasn't been 1977 for a long time.

Some treasures are genuine treasures. I know that and I'm not saying that truly meaningful mementos should be tossed out. I have a thank-you note from Richard Nixon—signed and everything—that says, "I extend to you my personal thanks and sincere appreciation . . ." I received it at the discharge center when I left the military service and I'm sure I was the only guy who got one. I wouldn't part with my Richard Nixon thank-you note for anything.

But I'm not too sure what I should do with my hockey stick, or for that matter, my tennis racket and bowling ball. I don't play hockey or tennis and I haven't bowled since I was 16, which was 26 years ago, which also happens to be when I bought the bowling ball. I've moved a lot since I was 16, and everywhere I move, the bowling ball moves, along with the hockey stick and the tennis racket.

Do you carry around stuff like that?

Some of it I've been talked into keeping. The friend who

helped me move into my house last year walked into the garage and said, "Look at that!" He pointed to a handleless, two-man saw blade hanging on a garage wall. "That's great. You should keep that," he said.

So I have. But I don't know why.

"And look at this!" he said (after he had talked me into keeping the two-man saw blade). He picked up a box of rocks, or maybe it was petrified wood, or rocks and petrified wood. I'm not sure; I haven't looked at them closely. "This is terrific!" he said. "You aren't going to throw this out, are you?"

Probably, I told him.

"Well, if you're going to throw it out," he said in that tone of voice generally used when talking to tasteless, culturally-deprived morons, "I'll take it."

As soon as he said that, I started thinking about every story I had ever heard about thrown-away junk turning out to be priceless works of art. So I kept the box of rocks as sort of an investment—a hedge against inflation. I store the rocks right next to the two cases of empty Pleasuretime Soda bottles. (Pleasuretime Soda went out of business last year. I think I'm keeping the empty bottles in case the business starts up again and I have a chance to get my deposit back.)

Besides, the bottles seem to be part of me now, which has to be the reason I keep all these things. It's got to be why everybody collects useless junk and would rather watch an all-political-ads television station than part with two cases of empty Pleasuretime Soda bottles. Who knows? In twenty years maybe they'll be just as valuable as bubble gum baseball cards are today. Naturally, I used to have a large collection of baseball cards, about 1,200 as I remember; and naturally, they're valuable; and naturally, when my mother called one day when I was well into adulthood and asked what she should do with them, I said . . . Never mind what I said. I don't like thinking about it.

Other things don't leave as easily. It took eight moves and many years before I could bring myself to toss out the decoupage pictures of a hockey player that a friend of mine made for me. Nobody I met liked that decoupage hockey player. After awhile, I grew tired of it, too, but throwing it away was every bit as painful as the day I parted company with a bamboo hanging of W. C. Fields which said, "Reminds me of my trip into the wilds of Afghanistan. We lost our corkscrew and had to live on food and water for several days."

"You've been out of college for a long time," a friend said. "Don't you think it's about time you got rid of that thing?"

A nasty argument ensued; two years later I gave in and threw it out. It still hurts.

A guitar I have never played leans against a desk that contains a swizzle stick from Caesar's Palace and a Riviera Hotel menu with a picture of Don Rickles on the front. I found the guitar at the city dump when I went there to throw away the decoupage hockey player. I've been meaning to take guitar lessons for fourteen years, but I never had a guitar. Now I've got one. I haven't taken guitar lessons yet, but at least the guitar has a home and I have another reminder of how good a guitar player I'd be if I ever got around to taking lessons.

I think I've figured out why I keep all that stuff. Some of it reminds me of past glories and nobody wants to throw out glories. Other junk reminds me of what might have been, or might be, and nobody likes to throw out dreams.

That makes sense—even if it doesn't explain why I'm still hanging onto a Hartz Mountain flea collar my cat will never wear.

41

Banana Republic

A lunch-hour question started the conversation: What qualities usually are identified with a banana republic?

"New Mexico," someone said, laughing. "At least geographically." He explained that banana republics always are south of the border, and in the minds of many Americans, that's where New Mexico is to be found.

A banana republic always has to be someplace exotic, a place Americans have vaguely heard of, but, when pressed, can't describe or identify with any detail. It has to be a place widely identifiable as belonging to a particular region, but not a place easily spotted on a map.

"Just like New Mexico," another lunchmate said, laughing again.

We decided a banana republic had to have a mild climate and be a place where many of the people spoke a language other than English, and in almost all cases that language had to be Spanish. The population had to be different from the American mainstream, so as to appear vaguely mysterious. A banana republic also would have to be a good vacation place and possibly, depending on other factors, a place where people might retire.

Again, someone laughed and said, "We're coming dangerously close to New Mexico again."

After awhile, we decided all these qualities, regardless of a New Mexico connection, went into the making of a banana republic. One essential quality, though was missing. Without it, no republic could lay claim to being a banana. All banana republics had to have unstable governments. Outsiders, be they other governments, businesses or potential investors, could always identify the banana republic by its inability to govern itself.

From the outside, the shaky banana republic government would be marked by paralysis, an inability to achieve anything constructive. Bitter pettiness resulting from the massive egos of government leaders, intent on protecting the small empires they had built for themselves, would prevent compromise, leaving the banana republic in a constant state of turmoil.

"It almost always leads to private armies, and at least private funding of governmental bodies, sort of like what some New Mexico legislators are suggesting for funding certain committees, but on a larger scale."

"Total breakdown of government facilities," said another. "The banana republic would be in such a state of disarray that government buildings, maybe even the capitol itself, would be shut down. Sort of like . . . well, like what could happen in Santa Fe, because of this last legislative session . . . but on a bigger scale, of course."

"Slit throats," someone else said, "but the throat cutters are cutting their own. For instance, in a banana republic, the government might be so bogged down in internal fighting that it could allow the educational system to collapse. Maybe the government would refuse to fund, or worse, by simple error, fail to fund institutions of higher education."

"More self-inflicted throat cutting," came another voice. "A lot of high-tech companies look to build and invest in what turn out to be banana republics. The true banana republic, during a period of stability, would woo these companies, fund centers for technological excellence and then, while the republic's leaders are preoccupied with internal bloodletting, let it all slip away. And even if they recover, it's too late; the damage is done. The high-tech investors will always think twice before they approach the banana republic again. It's sort of like what happened when the Legislature . . . well, you know."

"Does any of this sound familiar?" somebody asked. "Doesn't

this sound an awful lot like what happened in the last legislative session in—"

Just then the waitress appeared. "Dessert?" she said.

There was a moment of awkward silence. Then somebody answered for all of us.

"We'll have the special."

"OK," the waitress said. "Five banana splits. Santa Fe style. Coming right up."

42
A Monumental Act of God

LAS VEGAS—"Whoa! Hold it! Stop! Look at that! Look at that!" Robert Bluestone hollered.

The car slid to a stop in the mud of the road shoulder. Everything we could see through the windshield—the mountains, pastures, trees, the small lake—everything faded until the windshield seemed to fill with the bird.

The bald eagle, maybe one hundred yards away and seventy-five feet off the ground, cruised toward us. He began a lazy turn to the right of the car, banking around us. We scrambled out of the car, raised binoculars to our eyes and watched the eagle float by; the sun glinted off his outstretched black wings, the white head turned toward us, returning our gaze as he continued the long, slow turn over the grassland, down toward the icy surface of tiny McAllister Lake.

Robert Bluestone first called about a year ago. "Have you ever been to McAllister Lake?" he asked. "They seem to take over when the fishermen are gone." His second telephone call came a few weeks ago. "They're back."

We met at the classical guitarist's office in the music department of New Mexico Highlands University. After loading the car with jackets, binoculars and a telescope, we began the short drive to McAllister Lake. It is high plains country with the Sangre de Cristos providing a backdrop. Across the pastures, stripped-down, winterized cottonwoods popped up haphazardly. McAllister Lake was not yet in sight when Robert Bluestone said, "Stop the car."

I followed the instructions, but the reason for stopping was not evident. Nothing could be seen but the pastures, an occasional cottonwood and the blue sky that might explain why the earliest New Mexicans put such value on turquoise. Robert Bluestone says there are days when he comes to look for the eagles that the blue expanse makes him feel as if he were at the bottom of an ocean.

"See that cottonwood?" he said, pointing to a distant tree. "See that clump that doesn't quite fit the symmetry of the branches?" Binoculars came out. It was a bird. We got out of the car and set up the telescope tripod. Bluestone focused the telescope. "Ta-da!" he announced with suitable flourish. "I give you, posing as only he can, the great American bald eagle."

The eagle sat in the cottonwood as eagles sit on branches in zoo cages. Soon there came decidedly urban thoughts of the most-often-asked question of children at a zoo: Why doesn't he do anything? Why does he just sit there?

But this isn't the zoo. Eagles aren't required to entertain. No eagle sent us an invitation. If we are here, we are here only on his terms. Robert Bluestone likens it to the New Mexican land. You come to terms with it on its terms, not yours.

We took turns peering through the telescope.

"I felt as if I'm being let in on some sort of secret," I said. "It feels good just knowing they exist."

"What a momumental act of God," Robert Bluestone said. "That eagle, just sitting in that tree, justifies the need for wilderness. And I don't have to go there. I don't have to see it. It's enough for me that I know such a place exists."

The monumental act of God left the tree, his wings slowly providing lift. There was none of the flap-flap-flapping of lesser birds. Only long, graceful arcs, until he caught the warm, rising air and rode the thermal upward.

As the day wore on we stopped counting at six or seven eagles. Some cruised the thermals; others whiled away the afternoon in a cottonwood, watching geese honk by or the heavy, full-racked buck and five does lope across game-refuge pastures. Two hawks, initially mistaken for eagles, pirouetted in a high-altitude ballet.

It was late afternoon, no eagles spotted for hours, on our way home, when we were buzzed by the last eagle, close enough so the binoculars were nice to have but not necessary; this eagle was close enough for us to say, "No doubt about this one. This is no hawk."

The eagle made a slow turn around McAllister Lake. A gaggle of geese on the lake surface fidgeted. The eagle began another—lower—slow turn around the lake. This second cruise around the lake did the trick; the geese had had enough. In a honking riot, they rose off the ice and left. The eagle continued his circle, finally landing on the ice of the now gooseless lake.

We set up the telescope and watched him for ten or fifteen minutes, occasionally using the binoculars to scan the surrounding area.

Suddenly, he was gone. Neither one of us saw him leave. We scanned the lake, the sky, the pastures, the cottonwoods, back to the lake, back up to the sky.

He was gone, but it didn't matter. We knew he was out there somewhere.

43

Two Peas in a
Hospital Pod

Lewis Thomas and I are two peas in a pod. Lewis Thomas, physician-philosopher-essayist, is good for me and, I'd be willing to wager, good for a lot of other people. Lewis Thomas is an uninvolved patient, and so am I.

I do not know if an injection in between the facets of a joint is something to worry about. I don't care, either. I only know that my facet was not faceting (or whatever facets do) the way it should. (A facet is a small plane surface on a hard body, as on a bone. This one is somewhere near the bottom of my spine, and it is not faceting the way it should facet, and it hurts.) The night before my facet became an injectee, I read Lewis Thomas's collection of essays, *Late Night Thoughts on Listening to Mahler's Ninth Symphony*.

It helped when he wrote about the day someone inserted a pacemaker into his chest. The heart surgeon stood at the foot of his bed and said a pacemaker would do the trick, immediately, no delay. The surgeon wanted to know what Lewis Thomas thought about the idea. Lewis Thomas said it was one of those things to which a man was not entitled an opinion. This ball game was the surgeon's ball game, and Lewis Thomas wanted only to be a spectator.

Lewis Thomas was on my mind as I stood in the hospital X-ray room with its cabinets full of Star Wars props and its walls lined with machines of unknown origin and purpose. A slow, circular perusal confirmed that what we had here was 360 degrees of ignorance on my part—a full circle of technology to which I was not entitled an opinion. I decided it was just as well, comforting myself in the knowledge that there was a relatively small, finite number of machines to which they could hook me up.

I know this was wrong. I was being a bad patient. I have read many of the articles about being an involved patient. But I am all for limited involvement, just as Lewis Thomas has taught me to be.

He thought that as a reasonably intelligent doctor-patient he would ask intelligent, penetrating questions, make his own decisions, maybe even give step-by-step instructions to the surgeon. But it didn't turn out that way. It turned out he didn't want to ask questions, didn't want explanations, didn't want anything but the people who knew what they were doing to stop standing around waiting for questions and to get on with the job. He admitted that as a physician he was in agreement with the popular, magazine wisdom that said patients should be assertive and take more responsibility. But now he was a patient, and explanations weren't nearly as attractive as the prospect of something broken being fixed. So he told the surgeon to hold the talk and get on with the fixing.

I remember Lewis Thomas's words as the surgeon and X-ray technician turn me this way and that to get a better view of my spine—my spine the TV star, parading across a television monitor above the X-ray table.

"Well, I'll be darned," the doctor says. "Looks like a touch of spina bifida there."

This one I can't resist. All of a sudden I'm an involved patient. "What did you say?" I say.

He says "spina bifida" again.

This is not good. Spina bifida is big stuff. Lewis Thomas is momentarily cast aside. This calls for involvement.

"Do I have to worry about it? Does it need fixing? Do I have to protect it? When I stand in line at the movies, should I always let people move in front of me so I don't get whacked in the back?"

"No," the doctor says. "Don't worry about it. I think you'll be all right."

"OK, I won't worry about it. Don't fix it. Fix the other thing."

(The last time something big came along I didn't have Lewis Thomas to comfort me. Where was he several years ago when a dermatologist told me that what I thought was Clearasil-resistant zit was cancerous? The dermatologist fixed it, explaining that skin cancer among fair-skinned people in sunny climates wasn't so rare.)

The doctor completes the injection. We look at X-rays. He explains them. I nod in an Oscar-winning display of comprehension. "Uh-huh . . . Oh, sure . . . I see . . . Yes, of course."

Lewis Thomas acknowledges feeling guilty about his uninvolvement. I know how he feels.

"That should do it," my surgeon says.

Is it fixed?

"Yep."

Good. See you around.

44

Old Cowboys Don't Fade Away

Let's take a minute to see if we can sort this out.

• An 81-year-old rancher named Dave McDonald gathers together his niece, a 180-gallon water tank, cots, bedrolls, a suitcase, enough groceries for a month, two .30-.30 rifles and a .45 Colt pistol; then he drives onto White Sands Missile Range and reclaims the home the government kicked him out of in 1942.

So far so good. Now comes the hard part.

• An Army colonel, responding to the actions of Dave McDonald, says, "We have people who inadvertently come on our range periodically and we ask them to leave. Normally, they leave."

A lot of time could be spent trying to figure out how Dave McDonald accidentally equipped himself with a 180-gallon water tank, bedrolls, food, firearms, etc., and "inadvertently" drove onto the missile range. Let's not bother. I think the colonel is mistaken about Dave; I think Dave did the whole thing on purpose—which leads to the next question: Why?

It's been a few months since Dave McDonald reclaimed his ranch from the government. There was a flurry of publicity that now has faded. If the government thinks Dave McDonald has faded along with it, the government is as wrong as it was when it took his land. Some things don't fade, such as the memories of Tularosa Basin ranchers who, during World War II, acted like the patriots they were. They gave up their homes to the government, on the promise that they would be allowed to return or be fairly compensated. Neither has happened.

"Well, it was like being away from home for a long time, by gollys," Dave McDonald says of the brief time he reclaimed his ranch. "It felt right good out there. The thing you miss is your cattle. You raise 'em up, go out there every day, check 'em, see what's goin' on, you see. You just felt like, well, I don't know what . . . You just felt good about being out there."

He hadn't been out there since 1943. He's been living in a house in Socorro. He calls the house the "barn." Government might have trouble seeing the difference.

"You just don't want to go back to town after you've been out there," he says.

Government might not understand these things, just as it probably didn't understand Dave's brother, who, after putting up with the government in the 40s, Dave says, "decided to build himself another ranch. Then this Army man come up to him and said would you consider givin' up your place here. We want to run a line from here to there and take over some more land. My brother said he told that so-and-so 'I won't move another gaaawwwdam step and I'll use my gun before I'll move again.' "

Maybe this is a clue the government can use to see why the publicity may be gone but Dave McDonald isn't.

Maybe the government should ride along with this old rancher down the dirt road that goes deep into the rangeland.

The government should ride through the desert with Dave McDonald ("some desert, huh?"), past the yuccas, sage, broomweed, gramma grass, burroweed, salt grass, bunch grass, teaweed ("Makes a good tea; I've made lots of tea from that"), and clapweed ("That's what the cowboys called it, anyways"). Some of it cattle will eat; some of it cattle won't eat. Some of it is good for cattle; some of it isn't. All of it is alive, growing in this "desert."

Government needs to see the difference between its side and the range side of the steel-posted government fence, and then maybe government will begin to understand Dave McDonald. One side is grazed; the other isn't. The government side has yuccas with blooms; the other side has yuccas without blooms. ("Cows get up after 'em and eat 'em. Cow'll

shade under a yucca and chew all day, happy as can be.")
Dave McDonald says the government side is a fire hazard.

"They made it a fire hazard," he says, pointing at the thick, dry grass on the government side of the fence. "Took the cattle off and made it a fire hazard."

"Little by little, they're destroyin' us," Dave says. "I may be one of the few old people left and by gollys, they're tryin' to destroy us. Age us out. But, by gollys, I'll keep on fightin' 'em and when I'm gone, somebody else will. I say they're traitors to this country out here because they led people to believe it was desert and such stuff as that. It makes me bitter and I'm not ashamed to say it.

"This is beautiful country bein' wasted. Just wasted. What you're seein' on that government side of the fence is virgin land. That's what it amounts to now . . . virgin land. But they're goin' back. Those ranchers and their families are goin' back. You be sure to put that in your article. It's goin' to happen. It might be in five years or it might be in more, but by gollys, it's going to happen."

He pointed to the small tape recorder jammed between the front seats of the car.

"You make sure you get all that on that machine," Dave McDonald said.

45

Golfing with the Gods

The mountain doesn't have anything to do with my golf game. I know that. But the mountain is always there. It comes and goes, popping in and out of view, depending on the twists and turns of the small golf course near the airport.

But at the ninth tee you look west and you can see it clearly. It's a long way off, but dwarfs everything between the tee and itself. The volcanos on the West Mesa, the power poles, the highway, half a city, even the mesa itself, stretched out like a sandy-brown aircraft carrier with a flight deck reaching into infinity, all are insignificant lying in front of what we call Mount Taylor, and the Navajo—The People—call Tso Dzil, Turquoise Mountain.

I know I should not be thinking about a mountain while trying to learn the game of golf. The golf pro, a man of limitless patience, has tried to explain that a swing adequate for hitting a moving baseball falls short when trying to hit a smaller sphere, lying impudently motionless at my feet. He would give low marks to the novice who looks west toward the mountain, instead of down at the ball.

But it can't be helped. Maybe it's the dichotomy. The mountain means permanence. It signals stability. Everything around the ninth tee is transient.

Gibson Boulevard is a rush of motion and noise. To the south, 727s taxi behind a watery screen of heat waves. Even for those who rest, it is a brief stop at an airport hotel before they catch the next plane or rent a car and add to the carbon monoxide of Gibson Boulevard.

A friend who has spent time in Greece says Albuquerque reminds him of Athens.

"Take away the West Mesa and insert the Aegean, and it's not all that different," he says.

We drove through the mountains and he remarked, "Boy! What a great time the Greeks would have had making up stories about how these were made."

I said he was not the first to consider such a possibility. Then I asked him the same questions others have been asked, the same questions I asked of myself, because I don't know enough—and probably never will—about the mountain and what it means to its people.

Did he know that Tso Dzil is secured to the ground with a magic stone knife?

Did he know that the Holy People decorated it with turquoise, blue cloud, female rain and left Big Snake to guard it?

And if the Greeks wanted to tell stories about Turquoise Mountain, would they remember to include the spirit-body that stretches over the land bordered by Tso Dzil, Mount Blanco in the Sangre de Cristos, Mount Hesperus in the La Platas and the San Francisco Peaks above Flagstaff?

Would the Greeks fill that land with harmony?

If the Greeks wanted to move in their warriors, how would they move out the Hero Twins—Monster Slayer and Child Born of Water? When they slew the monsters and made the land safe, the battle began at Turquoise Mountain.

But these are not thoughts to be entertained while teeing up a golf ball. You can't think about Turquoise Girl, living on the mountain, guarding the country, while you're deciding whether to use your uncontrollable driver or your uncontrollable 2-iron.

So one day I left the golf clubs in the car and went back to the ninth tee. A foursome came to the tee shortly after I sat down at a nearby bench. They appeared, to use the polite word, to be retired. If you prefer bluntness, they were old men.

None had power in the muscular, Neanderthal sense. None would launch the ball into a whistling, 280-yard flight path.

There was power enough all around them. The cars whizzed up and down Gibson. The jets rattled eardrums and windows. The old men had none of this obvious kind of power. But they did swing effortlessly and smoothly, sending each golf ball on a straight course down the middle of the fairway. Each had an easy second shot.

I watched them walk toward the green, and the mountain. It seemed there was a connection, that the old men and the mountain had acquired a quiet power that allowed them to define limitations and identify the successes to be found within them.

Maybe that's what stops you for just a minute at the ninth tee, before you realize you can't spend all day thinking about a mountain held down with a magic knife. You've got to get back to the business at hand, back to driving down Gibson Boulevard, or catching a plane, or hoping that some Saturday when Monster Slayer has time on his hands and feels like doing battle with a great evil, he might decide to take a whack at your golf game.

46
Give Suzanne a Break

Ease off, friends. Give it some slack. Let's everybody calm down and give Suzanne Dundas a break. Suzanne Dundas wrote a letter to the *Journal*. The letter generated other letters; it even generated letters to me. Running through these letters was the theme that more or less suggested we put Suzanne Dundas on the first available train for El Paso or some other God-forsaken place. Surely, we can be more civil.

Here is part of what Suzanne Dundas wrote about Albuquerque: "The second most livable city in the United States: hah. I've lived in several different cities . . . and every single one of them has more to offer than Albuquerque, except one thing—unfounded conceit. Living in Albuquerque one year, I've heard how wonderful a city it is *ad nauseum*. But, when I ask what makes it so wonderful, no one seems to be able to tell me. Perhaps it's the innovative layout of the city—all major streets in a grid with every other intersection blocked off by construction. Perhaps it's the consistent architectural style of the city—fast food, pre-fab. Perhaps it's the desert air, which can block my sinuses quicker than molasses. Yes, Albuquerque has all this and more. Thank you, Uncle Sam, for assigning me here. I won't hate my three years here. But stop kidding yourselves. Albuquerque is just not that livable a city."

There's more, but you get the idea.

Upon reading this letter last week, my first thought was: Suzanne Dundas does not realize that Albuquerque is unique because it is the only major American city surrounded by New Mexico. My second thought was: People will respond unkindly to this. People will be unpleasant toward Suzanne Dundas because they don't understand her.

Unless you're a GI or an ex-GI, you won't have a handle on what's happening. The key to understanding is her statement: "Thank you, Uncle Sam, for assigning me here." This caused me to call Kirtland Air Force Base and inquire about Suzanne Dundas. Sure enough, she's a GI, an officer attached to the University of New Mexico ROTC unit. Under the most liberal interpretation of the phrase, this cannot be considered "tough duty," but it does help to explain why Suzanne Dundas is griping.

Individual rights we in civilian life take for granted are not afforded the GI, not even to an officer stationed at a university. In the military, these rights are not called *rights*. They are called court-martial offenses. There are a few GI rights, though, and one stands above all others in that slim volume known as the GI Bill of Rights. It is the right to bitch about where you are. It makes no difference where you are or what rank you hold, you are granted the free exercise of your right to bitch.

For instance, no one will dispute that one of the most glamorous spots in this great nation of ours is Oxnard, CA. I was stationed at Oxnard, and, hard as it is to believe, I complained. What appears to me now as a pleasant community with the ocean on one side and orchards on another, appeared to me then as a one-horse, hick town where there was nothing to do for fun except hang out at The Flapper. I once saw a young woman named Joannie Carson perform at The Flapper and she . . . Well, that's a story for another time.

I was stationed in England. I griped. Now I save nickels and dimes so I can go back.

I was stationed at the West Mesa radar site just outside of Albuquerque. The day I arrived, so did a sand storm. I griped. I bitched about the Mexican food, the dopey-looking houses, the wind, the barren brown land, everything. I even complained about the rattlesnakes and scorpions we found in the desert. Eventually, I griped myself to such a point of exhaustion that I was unable to move and have been living here ever since.

One of the cities Suzanne Dundas praised was Boston. A friend of mine recently returned from Boston. Boston is his home ground. He said, "I forgot that driving in Boston is nothing more than a simple, open act of aggression." Suzanne Dundas probably forgot that when she was in the throes of a Boston memory; one day she will be thankful for her stay in Albuquerque, where we are not in the least bit aggressive. We just don't know how to drive, that's all. When we have an accident, it is nothing more than an accident, an unintentional meeting of two vehicles. In Boston they call it a "score."

So everybody give Suzanne Dundas a break. Give her some time. Wait until Albuquerque is not where she is, but where she just came from. Wait until Uncle Sam plops her down on a Korean hilltop just this side of the 38th parallel and then ask her what she thinks about Albuquerque, New Mexico.

47

Perils of Poly Sci

Looking a gift horse in the mouth is bad enough, but why do so many people feel the need to shoot the thing in the head, too?

First, the good news: Joel Lieske, a Cleveland State University political science professor, has released a study showing Albuquerque to be the absolutely worst place in America for young families to set up housekeeping. This is marvelous. This is the greatest public service provided by a political science professor since 1972 when one of them told Richard Nixon that recent studies showed nobody in Congress had to nerve to impeach a president.

Now the bad news: The Cleveland study brought the usual shortsighted grousing from Albuquerque officials, boosters and other assorted hangers-on generally identified as "community leaders." (To be fair, they weren't nearly as bad as the boys in Tulsa, who threatened to sue the professor for libeling Tulsa, a virtually impossible feat, even for a political science professor.)

The typical Albuquerque complaint contained some insulting reference to Cleveland (a fine city where young families—or old families for that matter—might consider staying forever). Albuquerque officials asked, "What does some professor in Cleveland know? Who cares what he says?"

• What political science professors from Cleveland say is extremely useful—especially if they say it in Cleveland. Should a political science professor make an announcement of the recent sort in Albuquerque, it does us no good; however, as long as he stays in Cleveland, talking to Clevelanders, we're in fine shape. In the case of Professor Lieske, Albuquerque was blessed many times over because the story was spread across the land by the wire services. Think about the grand possibilities. Can't you see the headline in the *New York Post:* ALBUQUERQUE TO YOUNG FAMILIES: DROP DEAD!

• For reasons as yet unexplained, people in Cleveland still pay attention to what political science professors say. (The last recorded instance of this occurrence in New Mexico came in 1680, when a political science professor on his way to a seminar in San Francisco, stopped long enough to say, "Boy, the Pueblo Indians around here sure are a docile bunch, aren't they?")

• It goes without saying (which is a way writers have of saying something that doesn't have to be said, but is going to be said anyway), that this bad publicity might stop young families from moving to Albuquerque. A young Cleveland family, or Newark family, or New York family, might see the professor's study and decide not to move here. It could happen, but only if we're lucky.

Exactly why Albuquerque is such a terrible place for young families is unknown. I tried to call Professor Lieske at his Cleveland home, but the line was busy. After several hours, I quit trying, because it finally dawned on me that thousands of New Mexicans probably were jamming the lines to thank the man.

So I put my mind at rest about the professor and moved on to the next bit of good news. Albuquerque has been slammed by an authority far greater than a political science professor or some demographer or a Nobel Prize–winning sociologist or a game show host or even a disc jockey. We've been slammed by a rock star, and an old, on-the-comeback-trail rock star at that. In *Time* magazine, John Fogerty, former lead singer with Creedence Clearwater Revival, said that once you stop the next step is backward, and you're going to end up in a bar some place in Albuquerque.

What can we say? It's true. But at least it will be a quiet, relaxed bar, where a guy can go for a beer and not have to worry about being bothered by those young family types from Cleveland. We ran them out of town a long time ago.

48

The Writer

Mazie Mastromarino stands before the blackboard in the Technical-Vocational Institute classroom. On the blackboard are contractions: cannot—can't; could not—couldn't; do not—don't; did not— didn't; has not—hasn't.

"With contractions, we use the apostrophe," she tells the beginning English grammar class.

Rumbling blowers pushing air through the sprawl of T-VI buildings seems louder tonight. The adult students, numbering only two, are swallowed up by classroom trappings: desks, chairs, erasers, bulletin boards chaotic with announcements, and the clock, the round, institutional clock with its red sliver of a sweeping second hand—the kind of clock watched by millions of students and kept in time by only a handful of janitors who know the secret entrance to its innards. There aren't enough people in the room to cause the trappings to recede, to take a seat in the last row. Sometimes there are ten students in Beginning English Grammar, sometimes eight, sometimes six. Tonight there are two.

One is Margie Rodriguez. She is forty-eight years old and not yet a writer but is writing a book nonetheless. She promised to write it. She works all day, attends Beginning English Grammar class twice a week, and then comes home to write, sometimes a lot, sometimes a little. She wants to write this book, you see. She promised, and she wants to do it right.

"I have lupus," her daughter had said, "and you will write about it. It's just the three of us: you, me and the lupus."

Margie Rodriguez started the book a year and a half after her daughter died at the age of 18, after the systemic lupus finished the job of attacking the girl's major organs, infecting them, causing strokes in a child's body, and finally, eleven years after it began, killing Patsy. The writing did not go well.

"I tried writing then, but I couldn't," Margie says. "I made up my mind I was going to do it, but I wasn't ready. It was too soon. I had been mourning for the eleven years she was sick. I didn't think I had anything left to cry about. After a year and a half, I thought I would be ready. But I still had plenty to cry about. So I put it away."

Now it has been five years. She started writing a month ago, following her daughter's instructions: Don't write about the pain and hospitals and all that. Children with lupus know about that. Just tell how good life is. Tell how you have to learn to make the most of every minute you've got. Tell about how you can cope with the pain, and the faith you learn from it.

Margie Rodriguez says the book is for and about her daughter, and for children who know pain and disease. She doesn't want to inject herself into it. She doesn't want to write about her pain and the loneliness of ambulance rides in the middle of the night, of waiting alone in a corridor, waiting for a doctor to come out to say whether her daughter would live or die.

But the writing is tough.

"It's hard to do," Margie says. "Sometimes I look at what I write, scrunch it up in a ball and throw it away. I was ready to write, but I needed the commas and periods. One day my daughter-in-law said, 'Why don't you go back to school?'"

Margie Rodriguez, forty-eight years old, enrolled in Beginning English Grammar.

"Being in that class doesn't bother me," she says. "If you want to do something, you do it. I will keep on with it. I have made up my mind that I'm going to do it. And I'm going to do it. That's all there is to it. I will do it."

Mazie Mastromarino stands before the class and goes through the grammar exercises. Margie Rodriguez follows along in her workbook, looking up from time to time at her instructor. Tonight the lesson is on contractions.

49

Am I My Buyer's Shopper?

He doesn't shop. He buys. I don't shop, either. I buy. We are brothers in buyerhood. Shopping is not our cup of tea. We buy, and when we buy, we do it with a plan, such as: The Buy a Blue Shirt Plan. We enter the store and ask where the blue shirts are. We find them, find one that fits, buy it, and immediately leave the store. This might look like shopping, but it isn't. It's buying. It works all the time, every time, except Christmastime. Christmas forces us to shop.

Shopping is not the sort of thing we leap into blindly, or alone. It calls first for about an hour in the bagel place. The shopping center is nearly deserted at this time of morning. We should be planning our shopping trip, but we don't. We drink coffee, read the paper, talk about what we read in the paper, then debate about getting another raisin bagel with cream cheese. Raisin bagels with cream cheese always are preferable to shopping.

Eventually, though, the stores begin to open. I ask him how much time he has.

"Whole morning," he says. "She's watching the kids. I took care of them yesterday,. She's watching them today. But I did have to remind her I was going out to shop for her Christmas stuff before she agreed to stay with the kids all day."

What are you going to get her?

"I don't know."

Not even an idea?

"Well, yeah, I got a few ideas."

We're going to have to shop, aren't we?

"It looks unavoidable," he says with a sigh. "But whatever it is, it has to blow her mind. That's the whole idea, isn't it?

That's the fun. It doesn't matter what something costs. What matters is that you find something that's centered on the person you're giving it to."

He has a point. That is the best part. We will blow her mind, even if we have to shop to do it.

We wander through a large store, into the women's department, into what might as well be Mars or Jupiter for all we know. He looks at something . . . something sort of . . .

"What is it?" he says.

I don't know.

He holds the lingerie in one hand, looking it over. "You'd think they'd put instructions on these things or something."

A saleswoman comes by. "May I help you?" she says.

Yes, thanks, I say to her. We're looking for something somewhere between Norman Rockwell and Frederick's of Hollywood. (The saleswoman looks at me as if I just landed from Mars or Jupiter.)

"Do you know her size?" she asks him.

"Yeah, I've got that much."

"Good," the saleswoman says, "you're ahead of most of them who come in here."

But we don't buy anything. We move on, just looking around. We are shopping.

"How about this?" he says, holding up an item in another store. (You really don't expect me to say what it was, do you? It's a surprise, remember? Going to blow her mind, remember?)

Looks OK to me, I say.

"I like it."

Buy it.

He writes the check, gets a box from the saleswoman and then—in a moment of rare perception—summarizes the crucial difference between buyers and shoppers: "OK, that gets us out of this place."

We move on, picking up good stuff, stuff that will blow her mind. We are shopping, or at least doing what we think looks like shopping.

"Well, yeah, I like it, but, my God, her parents are here for Christmas. What are they going to say when they see it?"

"They come in purple and . . . what? What's periwinkle?"

How can they do it? we ask ourselves. How can shoppers, true shoppers, spend hours wandering around these stores? How can they spend all day in this merchandized cattle call? What's the attraction?

We stroll through another large department store, past outer clothes and under clothes, kitchenware and dinnerware, televisions, radios and stereos, round the corner through major appliances, and suddenly his eyes change. They are alive. He is taking in a whole section with a . . . a *shopping look*. He is shopping, really shopping; I can see it in his eyes. He wants to stay here all day, looking, touching, figuring out how much he can spend, or more probably not caring at all what anything costs.

He is shopping under a huge sign—HARDWARE—when he says, "I *know* I can find her some great stuff in here."

He runs his hand lovingly over a wood lathe.

"Boy, wouldn't this blow her mind?"

50

Jayjogging is Hazardous to Your Health

I almost hit him. I almost ran him down right in the middle of the street, almost squished him between the pavement and the front wheels of my Datsun. It was the noon hour, downtown. A large truck was ahead of me in the left lane of the one-way street; I was in the right lane. The truck slowed to a stop in the middle of the block. I slowed down. I don't know why. Just had a feeling that I should slow down. Then I slammed on the brakes.

And here he comes: T-shirt, shorts, running shoes, ears plugged into a tiny stereo. A jogger. He's stepping off in the middle of the block. Stopping a truck. Stopping me. Stopping everybody behind me and stopping everybody behind the truck in the other lane. Smiling at me and the trucker as he jayjogs across the street, up onto the sidewalk and down the block. Smiling all the way. Looking right at us and grinning.

It would have been tragic if somebody had run him down. Tragic, tragic, tragic. (All right, so it took me more than an hour to decide it would have been tragic. So who wants to make a snap decision about something such as this?) After belatedly recognizing this as a potential tragedy, I was left with a question to ponder: Why did this guy jayjog across a busy downtown street?

I know why he jogs. He jogs because it is good for him, which is fine with me. I have no quarrel with that. He jogs because jogging makes him feel good. No quarrel with that, either.

But why does he jayjog? Why does he step off the sidewalk in the middle of the street and jog into heavy traffic, bringing the traffic to halt while he, grinning like crazy, trots across to the other side? My guess is he jayjogs because he feels so good about jogging that he feels better than non-joggers, which is the problem. *Better* translates to *superior,* and that means he doesn't have to bother with those irritating little rules that prevent anarchy in the streets. In this case, the rules are traffic rules.

Traffic rules are for the lesser beings in vehicles, not for jayjoggers. Once jogging, the jogger does not stop. You've seen them at red lights where traffic was too heavy to cut through. The jogger stays on the sidewalk, running in place. Up-down, up-down, up-down.

I think this is done in order to stay loose, to stay warm, to keep the muscles limber. Either that or the guy is looking for the men's room. It's hard to tell.

But there's no doubt about why jayjoggers jayjog. They do it for the same reason non smokers preach to smokers and television evangelists preach to living rooms (and with any luck, living rooms equipped with rich widows). They are righteous. Can you imagine how bad it would be if a jayjogger got his own TV show and an 800 number?

In order to head off indignant letters, I want everybody to know I'm in favor of exercise, religion or anything else that makes you feel better. Did everybody hear that? Do I have to say it again? Maybe print it in italicized, bold-faced, upper-case letters? This is important, because whenever the righteous read something about their righteousness, a magic thing happens. When words appear that the righteous don't like, that's all they see. Everything else disappears.

I found out about this a few years ago when I wrote about bicycle riders who run red lights and give obscene hand signals to drivers who have the temerity to drive through a green light and then are forced to swerve to miss the red-light-running bike rider. So I wrote about bike riders. I commended bike riders for their practice of bike riding. I said they were smart to do it; it was good for them and didn't pollute the air. But I didn't say anything nice about bike riders who ran red lights and gave obscene hand signals to car drivers.

When bike riders read that column, all the friendly words disappeared. Poof! Just like that, all gone. The bike riders, unable to make a distinction between reasonable bike riders and unreasonable bike riders, fired off indignant letters about maniacs in cars who are always trying to run over bike riders.

I'm sure the same thing will happen with joggers, assuming such a thing as a reasonable jogger exists. Anyway, what I'm getting at is this: If you want to jog, go ahead and jog, but don't jayjog. Besides being rude, it's dangerous. You could get yourself run over.

Now, I'm not recommending that drivers run over jayjoggers. That would be wrong. I would never do anything like that. So don't run over jayjoggers, but if a jayjogger should cut in front of you, politely let him cross the street. Wait until he reaches the sidewalk and has run a few yards more. Roll down your window and yell at him. When he looks back to see who is yelling, he won't stop running, because joggers don't stop running for anything. With any luck, while he's looking back at you, he won't see that parking meter coming up a few yards ahead of him.

51
Uphill Skier

My toes were folded in half, the fronts kissing the backs in a painful perversion of the way nature meant toes to operate. My left knee, whose cartilage was ripped apart years ago in a football game, was twisted enough to recall the game, and even the surgery, with fondness. My neck was bent against the ground, my face mashed into the snow.

So this is it, I thought. After years of being coaxed, prodded, challenged and invited, I'm finally doing it. I'm skiing.

"Are you OK?" Richard asked.

Yes, thank you, I'm fine. How are you?

"Are you sure?" Richard's wife said.

When I twisted my head around to answer, I looked up at the sky, not because I wanted to, but because skyward was the only direction my head would point. Four eagles circled directly overhead through the gently falling snow.

"Eagles!" I hollered.

Richard and Marte looked at me strangely.

Using the arm that wasn't trapped under my body, I pointed to the sky.

"Eagles!" I hollered again.

The eagles slowly drifted in a tight circle. (I suppose they could have been buzzards, but that's not too romantic, is it?) After a few minutes they disappeared behind a snowy ridge. My companions politely took in more of the postcard scenery while I executed one of the more difficult skiing maneuvers: standing up.

I would like to say all of this happened as I was hurtling down the mountainside at sixty miles an hour, but I wasn't hurtling down the mountainside at all. I was, in fact, hurtling up the mountainside at a speed considered normal for the average pack mule. I was learning the fine art of cross-country skiing, and if I'm going to be brutally honest, I wasn't even hurtling up the mountain. I was almost standing still.

Early in the day I had mastered the art of falling down while standing perfectly still. We had skied about three-quarters of a mile and things were going well. I was high and dry. We stopped to look around. Someone behind me said something. I turned to talk, listed heavily to the port side and toppled to the ground, or at least to the snow covering the ground. Friends, when we talk about falling off skis while standing perfectly still, we are talking heavy-duty inelegance. My eagle-fall was made at least while movement was under way, even though it was minimal movement. (I wasn't going forward or backward. I was sort of standing in one place and trying to turn around.)

There is a crucial difference between falling down while standing almost still and falling down while standing perfectly still. Skiing came to me so naturally that I had mastered both at what the experts said was a surprisingly early stage.

Skiing at La Manga Pass seemed an unlikely place to spend the last day of 1984 and the first day of 1985, but the stillness was a nice departure from the usual New Year's riot. It made sense that maybe the best way to approach a new year is to quietly sneak up on it, rather than jolt it with too much booze and too many tinny noisemakers. The only sounds were the muted whisper of our skis gliding along the trail and the occasional soft crunch of a body tumbling into a snowbank.

On the first day, which was gray and snowy, I became acquainted with every conceivable form of skiing inelegance. The second day, during which I managed to remain upright and dry, was clear. The sun set the snow to sparkling and cross-country skiing began to make more sense.

No New Year's of mine had been celebrated like this one. It could become habit: the gentle sparkling snow, the stillness, the pines heavy with snow, dripping with icicles, and the authoritative grace of the eagles. (I don't mind starting the new year with my head buried in a snow drift, but nobody is going to persuade me that those birds were buzzards.)

52
Amtrakking

When the decision is made in Washington to derail
or not to derail Amtrak, the boy will not be called upon as
an expert witness. When Congress debates and committees
convene, the boy will not be summoned to testify on the
fundamental mystery of a train. The boy, and the mystery,
are much too emotional for the likes of a number-crunching
congressional committee. So the boy won't tell of the cloudy
afternoon he and I waited at the Albuquerque station, peering
down the tracks for the telltale light.

Once in a while, the boy turned his back to the southerly
tracks, letting his attention wander to the turquoise and silver
on the card tables set out by the jewelry sellers. Then the
thumping of traffic crossing the Lead Avenue overpass turned
him around, making him think the train was coming.

From the railroad platform, the sound of jets taking off
from the airport could be heard. In the train station neighborhood, it's a foreign sound, as foreign as the sound of the
word *jetway,* a twentieth-century, made-up word for a mechanical contraption passengers walk through to board air-
planes. Railroad passengers board from a platform, not a
jetway. *Platform* has a dependable sound to it; *platform* is
just as fundamental as the conveyance that will soon pull up
alongside it.

Across the tracks, transients lined up for a free meal. The
food was dispensed from a van. The men and women sat
down on a small, dusty incline to eat. The boy, who appeared
to be about eight years old, looked at them briefly, then returned his gaze to the southerly tracks. When I was eight, the
tracks weren't the Santa Fe's; the tracks, a block from my

house, belonged to the Rock Island and the B&O. Railroad tracks, even now, make me think of flattened pennies and pulverized rocks.

A conductor dressed in navy blue slacks, navy blue jacket with bright red trim on the buttonholes, black boots and a peaked cap climbed the steps from the station to the platform. He glanced at the boy and said, "Hi there, pardner," as he crossed the tracks and struck up a conversation with another railroad man.

The boy stood just inside the yellow line running parallel to the steel rails and wooden ties, ties engaged in more honest work than adding atmosphere to a back yard garden. From behind the boy came the voice of his mother. "Move away from the tracks," she said. "I hear the train coming."

The boy looked down the tracks. There was no sign, audio or visual, of the train. "OK," he said, backing up a few steps, and waiting for his mother to return to the station before he crossed the tracks to stand next to the railroad men. He stood there for a few minutes, his hands crammed into his pockets, just hanging around, killing time with the railroad men, chewing the fat and waiting for the Southwest Chief to roll into town.

His sister appeared on the platform. The boy crossed the tracks and talked to her while she tested her earphones and small tape player. She left and the boy's gaze returned to the distant tracks. Another sister appeared just as the engine light of the Southwest Chief came into view.

The boy pointed. "See?" he said.

"Yeah, I see," she replied, with a great show of disdain for the approaching silvery monster. (At times such as these the behavior of sisters borders on the sociopathic.)

The boy's hands came out of his pockets as the first rumbling sounds of the huge diesel engines could be heard. The Southwest Chief slowly pulled in. The engineer waved to the baggage handlers, then he waved to the conductor and the other railroad man. Then he looked at the boy, looked him squarely in the eye and smiled as he waved. The boy waved back.

Deep in my pockets, both hands twitched. One started to come out, but then relaxed and settled back into the pocket. The engine had rolled by and the dining car was coming up.

53

National Security Matters

While driving down Large River Boulevard, it occurred to me that this was going to take some time. I headed up the freeway, took the Saint Matthew exit, and by the time I cut over to Saint Pete, I decided New Mexico (or whatever we wind up calling it) could be in deep trouble.

The United States Constitution is nothing to trifle with. I called a lawyer. I asked about the proposed constitutional amendment that would make English the official language of America. If it's passed, I said, would it be unconstitutional to use any language but English?

The lawyer tried to stifle a chortle and said, *"Si."*

Are you telling me the next time I write a letter to someone in Santa Fe, I'll have to address it to The Royal Village of the Holy Faith of Saint Francis?

"Now you're getting the idea."

I won't have any room for the Zip code.

"Buy a bigger envelope."

Why is Spanish such a grave threat to the Republic?

"I'm not sure. Most of that information is classified. National security, you understand. An official language isn't the sort of thing you talk about carelessly. Remember: Loose (non-English-speaking unconstitutional) lips sink ships. But it must be important or nobody would be offering constitutional amendments to save the country. By the way, it's not just Spanish. It's any language but English. *Baton Rouge* and *Las Cruces* are in the same leaky linguistic boat. For instance, your use of Large River Boulevard is incorrect. *Boulevard* is a French word. What you need is Large River Street or Large River Lane."

But won't life be bland? It would be like an *enchilada* without *chile*.

"You better watch the way you talk."

Sorry. Is it OK if I say red or green?

"As long as nothing but *pepper* follows it."

Maybe I should think about this for a while. I'll go home, mix myself a *margarita*—

"Be careful."

Oh, I see . . .How about a gin?

"You're in compliance with gin."

OK, I'll pour some gin, go out on the *patio* and—

"No, you won't. Not unless you want to break the law. It would be a baldfaced violation of the Constitution for you to go out on the *patio*. Go out in the courtyard and you're all right. By the way, did I tell you about the house I'm building?"

No.

"We're putting a place out in Cattle Yards."

Cattle Yards?

"It used to be called *Corrales,* but now it's Cattle Yards. Anyway, we're building a house out there."

Adobe?

"Nope. Sun-dried mud brick."

Sun-dried mud . . .? Oh, I get it. Why are you moving? Tired of living in Albuquerque?

"Not exactly. Albuquerque's not so bad when you consider nobody lives there."

What?

"Can't have people living in a non-existent place, can you? What I'm tired of are the 350,000 souls living in Duke."

Duke? Oh . . .

"I'll miss the shopping, though. When I need something, it's so easy to whip over to one of the Winrocks."

Winrocks?

"East and West. No more—"

Coronado.

"You're catching on."

I guess this mean *Tijeras Canyon* will become Scissor Canyon, doesn't it?

"I'm not sure. *Tijeras* definitely is out, but canyon is tricky. Canyon is English for *cañón*. I look for that one to go all the way to the Supreme Court."

Surely, I won't have to rename my dog, will I?

"What's the dog's name?"

Dulce.

"Is she sweet?"

Yeah, a real doll.

"You'll adjust."

I suppose I will. Well, thanks for the help. Hey, are you doing anything Saturday?

"Nope."

Want to play some golf?

"Sure. Where do you want to play?"

Arroyo del Oso.

"Never heard of it."

54

Quiet Conversation

After the class, Phyllis Wilcox said, "I hope it wasn't uncomfortable for you."

No, I said, it wasn't uncomfortable. A little odd, maybe, but not uncomfortable. Maybe because the feeling wasn't unfamiliar. Something like it had happened before. It happened in Europe, Southeast Asia, and even a few times in New Mexico. It happened everywhere I had been where I didn't speak the language, everywhere I had been where I was on the outside.

The University of New Mexico surroundings were familiar enough, although some of them I hadn't noticed before. Of all the times, of all the thousands of times I walked from class to class on that campus, I never thought of the squawking crows or leaves being crunched underfoot or the tick-tick-tick of a 10-speed's rear wheel. I never thought of them being so much a part of me, and me being so much a part of them.

After I left the din of a university hallway in between classes and entered the silence of Phyllis Wilcox's classroom, I would think about crows and leaves even more.

This classroom silence is not the standard classroom silence. It is not the silence that slowly makes its way through the room when a professor enters, patiently quieting the talkers until he clears his throat or writes on a blackboard or whatever it takes to make the silence complete.

This silence is not a goal—it's the starting place for everything that is to follow. Silence is the prime rule, typed at the top of a handout: "VOICE: Forbidden." It makes all the sense anyone could ask for: If you are to learn to speak to someone who is deaf, you don't talk, at least not with your voice.

Everybody in the room is able to talk, even the two who are deaf. One of the deaf speakers is a student, the other is Phyllis Wilcox, the professor. All can talk, but none do.

A few minutes before Phyllis arrived I went in and took a seat in the back row.

"I'm sorry," a student would say later. "We thought you were deaf and had come to visit the class."

That explained the greeting, a sort of cheery military salute given with a smile. Then came the hands, flying through the air like so many tongues attached to the ends of arms. All kinds of greetings—lots of smiles, but only one smile (mine) feels like the grin of an idiot—one one face (mine) lights up in the embarrassed flush of an outsider.

Lots of hugs, too, but I don't even figure that one out. It isn't until after class that Phyllis explains. "If you want to get the attention of a deaf person, you don't yell at him," she says. "You could stamp your foot on the floor and maybe he would feel the vibration, but that would be rude. So you have to touch him, and in our society, touching is something we generally don't do. So I have the students hug. It helps break down the hesitancy to touch."

Anyone who has been in a non-English-speaking country knows about yelling. Americans have a tendency to holler at those who don't speak English, the theory being that increased volume will result in increased understanding. As is the case with other foreign languages, it doesn't work here, either.

Hands fly, eyebrows arch, facial gestures are exaggerated, and there is laughter. Somebody has cracked a good joke. Everybody laughs, except the outsider, who sits in the back row, grinning, uncomprehending.

It doesn't take much to reverse the picture, to make the outsider deaf in a world of sound. It doesn't take much to see why any group of outsiders would form a bond, united by their differences, forming their own society.

Phyllis Wilcox says the deaf world is a closed one, open only to its full-time members; it is a society to which she, even though deaf, does not belong. In spite of her deafness, she speaks articulately and operates well in the world of sound. She has moved from the core of the silent society.

For seventy-five minutes, the only sounds (other than laughter) come from outside the classroom: diesel engines, the crows, voices of passing students. Inside, eyes and hands make it clear that it is next to impossible to hide behind words in this language.

Phyllis introduces me to the class and one by one they introduce themselves and greet me. I want to acknowledge the greetings, but I don't. I am in the position of someone who knows little or nothing of the local customs. I begin thinking about a friend who, in the early days of her Spanish studies, met a man from Mexico. "Hello," she said in Spanish, "I am ripe. How are you?"

All I do is smile, and wonder what in the world they are saying to me.

Fourteen young people with expressive hands and expressive faces try to take a small step from the outside to the inside, knowing full well they will never reach the core of the society they approach. They are taught by one who says she has been at the core, but moved away from it.

And the only thing that seems certain is that no matter how far they go, they will go with little fanfare. They will go silently.

55

Blowing in the Wind

It's spring, and my fancy turns to antihistamines. I know it's spring because I'm paying close attention to the post-nasal-drip commercials. If you play the stock market, call your broker and tell him to buy Kleenex.

The winds are back. You probably noticed, didn't you? Driving down the freeway with a stranglehold on your steering wheel reminded you, didn't it? When the trees creaked and bent, sending branches scraping along the side of your house or across the roof so it sounded like the Eldorado marching band was up there practicing, you thought, *Ah, spring!*

Springtime in this town should be optional; there should be a way of putting a check mark next to the survey answer that says, "Not this year, thank you. I'd just as soon go directly to summer."

Give me heat, cold, rain, snow, sleet, ice . . . give me another legislative session . . . give me the collected speeches of Les Houston to memorize . . . give me anything but the wind, and the dust, and the . . . the what? There has to be something other than just the wind that's doing this to me. The wind can't be responsible by itself. I want to know who else is in the game. Who's responsible? Who's doing this to me? Don't everybody just sit there. Somebody own up to it.

Juniper? It is you? You had a pathetically high count yesterday in the pollen chart. How about cottonwood? Mold? Mulberry?

Something's got my sinuses leaking like the Bernalillo County courthouse plumbing. Something's making me feel as if there's a fifteen-round cat fight going on in my throat.

Every day I check the pollen count. It's right there on the weather page between the Pollution Index and Amsterdam (52 and 43 with rain).

Every day I look. Is it grass? Mulberry? Is that what's settled in my nose? Is it—I really don't like to think about this—is it insect parts?

Oh, God . . . insect parts.

It couldn't be ambrosia, not the food of the Greek and Roman gods. The dictionary says ambrosia is something extremely pleasing to taste and smell. The dictionary says ambrosia is a dessert of a fruit or mixed fruits topped with shredded coconut. The dictionary also says "see RAG-WEED."

No, I won't. I refuse to see RAGWEED. I'm not up to it. The print is too small and my eyes already feel like bloated Ping-Pong balls. I'd rather sulk. I won't curse the darkness, but I'll gladly do it to the wind.

In some parts of the world, the kind of wind that blows through here is used—successfully—as a defense against murder charges. Tired of hubby's chronic griping? Had a bellyful of wife's complaints? Go ahead and do the deed, but before you do, remember to call the National Weather Service to check the wind.

On television the other night I saw a report on the large number of orange barrel street construction barriers that are run over, squashed, demolished, shot, burned, destroyed with baseball bats and otherwise treated unkindly by the residents of this city. The report was too early. The report needs a few more weeks of this wind to see just how destructive we can be.

I don't know anyone who has a kind word to say about the wind. I don't know anyone who enjoys staying home all day and all night while Arizona passes through on its way to Texas. Kind words about the wind are hard to come by.

But come Sunday night, no doubt, when I punch up my public television station to watch "The Living Planet," David Attenborough will be waxing poetically about the windy sexual escapades of this spore and that seed. It's the right time of year for that sort of thing, but I'm not going to be in the mood for airborne orgies. I've got nothing nice to say about the wind and I sure don't want to listen to some British anthropologist rattling on about the miracle of life borne on the breeze.

Besides, I'd be willing to wager six boxes of Sinutabs that he doesn't say a word about the miracle of insect parts.

56
Baseball

Let's talk about baseball. Let's talk about why it's the best game. Baseball talk comes easy for me. I've been playing baseball, or talking about playing baseball, or talking about other players playing baseball for almost as long as I can remember. My career in baseball talk began in 1948, when I was four years old. It was a year marked by only two events that I can remember, one being my father taking me to my first big league game in Chicago (the White Sox beat the Indians), and the other being the birth of my sister—an event which justifiably ranked a close second to the White Sox beating the Indians.

So let's talk about baseball, because talk is what baseball is all about. In the first six words of his book, *How Life Imitates the World Series,* Thomas Boswell correctly observes that "Conversation is the blood of baseball." To get the blood circulating, I have to talk about the old men first. Whenever I hear the word *baseball,* I think of the old men I grew up with on the South Side of Chicago at 35th and Shields, Comiskey Park—Home of the White Sox. We belonged there; in a sense, lived there. It was ours, all of us: the players: Nellie Fox, Minnie Minoso, Sherman Lollar, Billy Pierce, Jungle Jim Rivera; the old men; me. I was never at a game more than ten minutes before I was talking to somebody, which is a natural, always-expected occurrence at all baseball games. More often than not, I talked with one of the old men. They knew so much. They had seen so much.

I still see them, no matter where the game is being played. I remember a Sunday afternoon in the Albuquerque Sports Stadium, watching the Dukes, the Los Angeles Dodgers Triple

A club. I sat in the grandstand next to an old man. I had never seen him before, didn't know his name, didn't know a thing in the world about him. Yet I almost said, "It's been awhile. How have you been?"

We talked baseball. We talked before the game, during the game, and after the game on the way to the parking lot. Sometimes the conversations were long and detailed; other times they were mercifully brief, especially the time a third baseman booted three consecutive ground balls, three consecutive *easy* ground balls. With each error the old man rolled his cigar from one side of his mouth to the other, hitched his suspenders a little, and finally shook his head slowly as he said, "Maybe he can hit."

Time permits conversation—the blood of baseball. It's not time in the quantitative sense, though. Measure baseball's time in numbers and you'll find it isn't all that different from any other sport. It's the same amount of time, but that's not the proper measure. You have to consider the quality of the time, you have to take into account what happens in that time. And what happens is confrontation.

Picture this: It's the bottom of the ninth, two outs, the pitcher has a one-run lead, the bases are loaded, the count on the .347 hitter is three and two. The pitcher has to throw the ball. The hitter has to respond. Put a football player out on that pitching mound and he'd fall down, clutch the ball to his chest and wait for the clock to run out.

Right up there with confrontation is accountability. No other team game has the accountability of baseball. Nobody can hide on a baseball field. Players in other games can hide, but not baseball players. Who really sees everything watching football or basketball or hockey? Too much is a blur, too much goes by unnoticed. Who really sees everything? I once heard a retired professional football player complain because the officials now announce the jersey number of an offender called for a penalty. He complained because he wasn't used to accountability. Not being accountable probably would appeal to baseball players. Or for that matter, anybody else, no matter the job. Wouldn't Mike Schmidt be happy if nobody knew who missed that third strike? Wouldn't Carlton Fisk enjoy his work more if nobody could figure out who sailed that throw into center field? You've got to worry about such things in baseball. You're out there for everybody to see. You can't hide. When the shortstop tries to catch a ball with his ankle instead of his glove, he can't point to the second baseman and say, "He did it, not me."

Throw in democracy, too. You don't have to weigh 265 pounds to play baseball. You don't have to be 6'9" and wear size 13 EEEEEE sneakers to play baseball. Skill is the equalizer. In football, only certain positions are called "skill positions." In baseball, all of them are.

Right along with accountability, confrontation and democracy is accessibility—although the builders of modern-day, multi-purpose stadiums seem intent on driving accessibility into extinction. Fortunately, that is not the case at the Albuquerque Sports Stadium, where the cheap seats are right on top of the field.

Baseball is supper at the kitchen table. It's not dinner in the dining room. That's too formal. Dinner in the dining room is more like golf. Baseball isn't a fast-food joint with burgers and fries that fill you up and are soon forgotten. That's football. Baseball is supper at the kitchen table with everybody talking: sometimes in low voices, sometimes loud, sometimes allowing a point, sometimes arguing like hell, sometimes tense, sometimes explosive. But always talking, and always comfortable.

I suppose being comfortable implies being an insider. I have heard baseball called an insider's game. Maybe it is. Maybe there's something about it, something so cosmic, that no matter how much you talk or write about it, the explanation remains elusive. For proof, I offer the cosmic statement of an old friend. He's forty-two, a softball player and a tennis player, but tennis is a new game to him. He says he plays tennis only because he knows the day is coming when he will have to stop playing softball. He doesn't look forward to it, but he wants another game to play when that day comes. So he plays tennis. When I saw him last, it was at a softball game. He stepped to the plate and ripped a screaming line-drive single to right field. When the inning ended, he came over to the bench, smiled at me, and delivered his cosmic statement: "I can't tell you why, but that feels better than 40-Love."

Of course it does. Baseball is the best game.

57

Candy Lady

Try as I might, I cannot find a light approach to this subject. Humor fails with this subject. Sadly, it is no laughing matter. So don't expect a smile, don't expect a laugh, don't expect so much as a smirk, because today we talk about sex, serious sex. Today is no laughing matter. Today is pornographic peanut clusters.

This story involves a businesswoman, the Albuquerque Zoning Enforcement Department, the Albuquerque Police Department, the city's chief administrative officer, the zoning administrator, the city attorney, the American Civil Liberties Union (if it's about sex, the ACLU always finds a way to get in the picture), and the Bible thumpers who can define obscenity but can't spell it.

At the center of the issue is Debbie Dorbandt, owner of the Candy Lady, an Old Town sweets shop. Among Mrs. Dorbandt's wares is X-rated candy, the sort of thing people buy as a joke for wives, husbands, boyfriends and girlfriends.

But this is no joke. This is sex. It's nothing to laugh about.

Our story begins with the Zoning Enforcement Department, one of those governmental agencies that must respond to the electorate, even if the electorate has chewy nougat where its brains are supposed to be. The department received a complaint about chocolate-covered prurience. The department went to Old Town and bought some, but strictly as evidence. I'm sure no one laughed, smiled or even smirked.

Then discussions began among the chief administrative officer, the zoning administrators, the city attorney and others with better things to do. The question: Do we or don't we remove this cream-filled menace and thwart a life of cinnamon red hot sin?

Mrs. Dorbandt, now an official alleged nuisance, contacted the American Civil Liberties Union, where cinnamon red hots are ordered in bulk.

Meanwhile, the city fathers decided Mrs. Dorbandt was not in violation of any regulations.

End of story? Don't bet your Whitman Sampler on it. Enter the North Valley Gospel Church.

One church member protested at the candy store and was pinched by the cops. Later, more protesters gathered, more cops gathered, TV cameras gathered, reporters gathered. They investigated Mrs. Dorbandt, they interviewed Mrs. Dorbandt, they filmed Mrs. Dorbandt, they protested Mrs. Dorbandt, and I figure Mrs. Dorbandt received approximately three years worth of free advertising, something the protesters probably didn't count on, but free advertising is a risk inherent to the protest business.

Although the crime statistics for the period involved are not available, chances are the Bible thumpers could have protested murders, rapes, assaults and burglaries. Instead, they found busty bon-bons more thump-worthy. One carried a sign that said "Pornography & Obsenity Is Sin." So is misspelling, and so is using the wrong verb. They're enough to make your M&Ms melt in your hands.

Mrs. Dorbandt, now established as a purveyor of devilish divinity, was no longer an alleged nuisance. She was official, the result of tangling with organized government and organized religion. Mrs. Dorbandt did not protest in the streets. She did not harass citizens. She was not arrested for anything. (Even the casual observer will recognize these as the common traits of a nuisance.)

We will leave it to the computers to figure out the number of hours spent on this case by police officers, attorneys and high government administrators. The figures will give us a price tag to hang on this grave threat to the community's well-being.

In the meantime, we have but one question to ponder: If the candy problem was that serious, if the candy was that much of a threat to Albuquerque's well-being, why the hell didn't somebody call a dentist instead of the cops?

58

The Hotel Hotel

Hardly a day passes that I don't look around the building in which I work and see people I don't know. I suspect the same thing happens to most people in their places of work. We are growing; new people are coming in.

Nothing is quite as intimidating as a new job in new surroundings, where, as everyone who has ever had a new job knows, the first piddling mistake will result in immediate firing, or at least a boss who wonders out loud, "He sure looked a lot better on paper, didn't he?"

So I want to help. I want to come up with an easily remembered, concise bit of advice, advice that will make the newcomer to New Mexico a little more comfortable, a little less easy to spot as an outlander.

Here is my advice: Don't say Rio Grande River.

If you say Rio Grande River, you immediately identify yourself as not even semi-bilingual (which means you don't speak Spanish, but you've picked up enough to fake it so everybody thinks you've lived here since 1958).

When you say Rio Grande River, expect condescending smirks, because when you say Rio Grande River, you're saying Big River River. Stick to Rio Grande, and remember that you are living in New Mexico, not Los Angeles, where you can say "the La Brea tar pits" and get away with it.

Los Angeles Times columnist Jack Smith says bilingual purists in L.A. continually zap him for using the English article *the* before the Spanish article *el* or *la* when they are used with proper names. When he writes about the La Brea tar pits, a purist invariably lets him have it for saying "the the Brea tar pits." The purest purists then point out that what he's really saying is "the the tar tar pits," because *brea* means *tar*.

Jack Smith says these slip-ups are common Californian errors, which makes them idiomatic, and therefore no big deal. He is a wonderful columnist, and he is correct with his idiomatic argument, and he also is in Los Angeles. Albuquerque is not Los Angeles (although from time to time we seem to be taking a real shot at it), and it is not in California (that I'm sure about).

At any rate, don't say Rio Grande River, and don't talk about the La Fonda Hotel in Santa Fe, unless you really mean to talk about the The Hotel Hotel. Same goes for La Bajada, that long climb into the sky south of Santa Fe; unless you mean to say The Hill Hill, don't say La Bajada hill, say La Bajada. Some purists will argue it means the "going down place" or "incline" or something like that. Don't worry about the purist. A hill by any other name is a bajada.

Jack Smith says the use of *el* and *la* is likely a purist affectation, and maybe it is in Southern California, but I'm not so sure about New Mexico.

Whether any of this will make you a purist is questionable. I'm not a purist, but I still like the idea of using *el* and *la* properly. *El* and *la* may be niggling little details, but they at least remind me that I am not living in Iowa or Kansas. *El* and *la* are dehomogenizers, reminding me that I live in a place that's different from the mainstream, and some of the reasons it is different are niggling little details such as *el* and *la*.

El and *la* remind me that a lot of history and a lot of people preceded me, and I can't get over the feeling that those people and that history need to be preserved.

After I've driven up and over The Hill to Santa Fe, *el* and *la* are the kinds of little details that remind me of where I am when I'm sitting in the bar, enjoying a cool one at The Hotel Hotel.

59

Valentine

Of all the western states I love New Mexico best
—Edward Abbey.

When New Mexico checks the mail today, it won't be faced
with the same problem Charlie Brown has in Peanuts. New
Mexico's mailbox always is stuffed with Valentine's cards.
Some of the cards are store-bought, with the schmaltzy plat-
itudes of a tourism brochure. Some are beautifully crafted,
written by the likes of D. H. Lawrence and Oliver La Farge.

I know a lot of people who have sent Valentine's cards to
New Mexico.

One fell in love while making practice bombing runs over
the Tularosa Basin in World War II. When the war was over,
he returned and came to know the basin on the ground. He
wrote about it, wrote about it again, set a prize-winning novel
in the basin, and then wrote about the great expanse yet again.
He won't tire of this. He's in love.

I know a woman who, every once in a while, gets in her
car and leaves Albuquerque, just because there are so many
places to leave to. She says, "Sometimes I just have to get out
there." She, too, is in love.

I know a musician who goes into that New Mexico vastness
because he says it's "calm." He says he needs it. "Maybe it's
because I play so many concerts," the classical guitarist says.
"Maybe it's because I spend so much of my time getting into
myself. Out here I can do it."

I know a woman who came here from New York. "New
York has everything," she says. "It has art, theater, music,
museums. Everything. But it's all being done *for* you. Here,

in the mountains, in the desert, there's more, but you have to find it. Nobody's going to do it for you."

I know a guy who had a houseful of in-laws. He liked his in-laws, but he said a day came when he absolutely, positively had to be alone. So he drove south on I-25, turned right on a two-lane road near Los Lunas and soon he was alone.

I know another guy who simply says, "This land puts me at rest."

These people all are sending Valentine's cards. One more can't hurt, so I think I'll send one, even if it does have the look of a homemade, smudged heart drawn by a third grader.

This card will have a picture of me returning from a vacation, staring through the small airplane window and suddenly realizing we are flying over New Mexico and there seems to be more space in the sky, even though the sky is crowded with cumulus clouds—those towering stacks of white that look like the debris to be found after an explosion in a meringue factory.

My Valentine's card will have a picture of that series of hills on NM 44, just past the Bernalillo Circle-K, where the rolling desert gives way, in about one-fifteenth of a second, to arroyos gouged in the red earth and mesas as far as you can see.

Open the card and on the inside is that two-lane road that goes east to Los Lunas and west to as far as you care to take it. It goes past ranch land, malpais mesas with desert life rooted in and crooked paths worn deep and jagged by a few million years of running water. This road goes all the way to Mount Taylor—where gods live.

There will be a drawing of me, sitting in my truck at the intersection of Lomas and Louisiana, waiting for the turn arrow. I will be looking west, right down Lomas, all the way to the mesa, thinking that even smack in the middle of the city New Mexico is always around, always reminding me that there are places close by to get away from the intersection of Lomas and Louisiana.

On the card I'll write the words of my friend: "This land puts me at rest."

That would be a nice thought to write on my Valentine's card to New Mexico—except for one small problem: That's not my Valentine's card to New Mexico. That's New Mexico's Valentine's card to me.